GOURMET TEAMWORK

Recipes to inspire engagement, improve business
processes, and make hybrid work sustainable with
Microsoft Teams (and the rest of Office 365)

Paul Woods, Helen Blunden, Aditi Gupta,
John Tropea, Jeff Bell & Jenni McNamara

Published by Rapid Circle
https://www.rapidcircle.com

Printed on demand in Australia, United States and United Kingdom
Set in Palatino Linotype
Edited by Cathryn Mora – Change Empire Books

Paperback ISBN: 978-0-646-85946-0

Paul's Dedication
To Kerrina, Gabby and Maddy

Helen's Dedication
To Andrew, my husband, who keeps telling me to write a book;
well, here's two of them now.

Aditi's dedication
To Rafael, my husband, and Ashish, my brother – my two
pillars of strength, and my team at Rapid Circle who encouraged
me to fulfil my dream to write a book! Affectionately to my
parents, Anil and Renuka, for always loving me and never giving
up on me despite my eccentrities!

John's dedication
To Mareesa and Denali, my two-favourite people in the
world. To my work and my projects, thank-you for being so
interesting, book-worthy actually ;)

Jeff's dedication
To all the people who travelled in and out my door, I'm glad
they came along to help me grow. To my wife Alana, I dedicate
my words to you.

Jenni's dedication
To my beautiful friends and family who have always believed
in me and allowed me to stretch my wings, and to my colleagues
and clients who have sometimes pushed me over the edge, just so
I could fly.

CONTENTS

PREFACE

After hearing about the future of work for what felt like eternity... the future of work has finally arrived. After years of predicting the demise of the daily commute, and the vacating of expensive commercial real estate around the world... all it took was a global pandemic to press the reset button on the way we work.

To be honest, I think we all would have preferred a more subtle kick into our 'new normal' (okay, sorry, I promise that is the last COVID-cliché you will get from this book!). The outbreak of COVID-19 across the world has impacted so many. So many lives, so many jobs, so many businesses. Through the disruption we have seen amazing stories of compassion, love, and support. Where teams, organisations, and communities have come together to serve in a time of need. We have also seen heartbreaking scenes as people raced to get back to their home country, where people have fought for their lives, and for far too many, where people have left us too soon.

Whether you or a loved one have been impacted by COVID, or you and your family have been impacted by the downstream effects of the pandemic (for example, business shutdowns, job losses, and border closures)... the only thing we can trust is, that eventually, one day, COVID will be behind us, and as a global community, we will recover.

For those working on the frontlines, the work of nurses and doctors, shop assistants and checkout operators, teachers and lecturers, and public officials from all levels of government, the impact of the pandemic was clear to see. Some saw their workload double overnight, whilst others were furloughed or let go. Many needed to reimagine how they did their jobs; with constraints they had never faced before.

Behind the scenes, support staff, management, and those you would class as 'knowledge' or 'information' workers saw an impact as well. In workplaces around the world, people were starting to feel the strain of trying to adjust to the new world. Offices around the world shut down as social distancing and community curfews were put in place. Managers of teams struggled to keep their teams connected. In almost all cases, managers relied on the constructs and expectations of 'the office' to structure how work occurs, and how their team performed.

Without 'standard hours', bookended by hours in traffic, or a physical workplace where they could eyeball each employee whenever necessary to ensure they are 'on task', many managers resorted to what looked like the path of least resistance. The video meeting. Many managers around the world had the same thought in their minds – "If I can see my staff, and my staff can see me, and we keep talking, we can remain connected over the next few weeks. And once this is all over, we can all come back into the office and get back to work for real."

Except… it wasn't just a few weeks.

In most cases, managers simply replaced what were face to face interactions, with video calls. And lots of them. It was at this moment we all realised that we are involved in far too many meetings. Before 2020, having back-to-back meetings was seen by many as an important signal of value (or realistically, busyness) at work. Back then, between meetings we still got a chance to duck to the rest room, swing past the coffee machine for a quick refill, or need to shuffle yourself and your laptop and notes to another meeting room.

Back-to-back meetings via video is another thing entirely. Reducing our switching costs between meetings to zero, with the next meeting literally one click away, meant that we started to pay the price. Screen fatigue became a real thing for millions of knowledge workers around the world. The business world flocked to a synchronous or real time way of keeping things going. Whilst this 'brute force' approach to communication, collaboration, and coordination worked well to begin with, cracks started to emerge when people felt more burnt out and were working longer hours than before the pandemic.

Personally, I felt it too. At Adopt & Embrace (now part of Rapid Circle – a COVID business acquisition story I will tell you later in the book), one of our core values is "work is a thing you do, not a place you go." To be honest, initially the impact of COVID on the way we do things was minor. We all regularly worked from home prior to the outbreak, so for us it was really business as usual. For those of us who usually split our time between working from home, and working from our local co-working space, we cannibalised some of the docking stations, LED monitors, and web cams that we used in town, and set ourselves up at home with a bit more equipment to help us better serve our customers. We made the decision to stop going into the co-working space about two weeks before most businesses started to encourage work from home… and got a lot of strange looks from passers-by as we lugged our monitors home on the bus or train.

Our early move meant that we were ready to support our customers across Australia and New Zealand when the lockdowns started to come into effect. We were able to help several universities and school districts transition to online learning. We helped a hospital to keep engaged with its nursing students so their learning was not disrupted (and they could graduate into what must be a challenging baptism of fire as a first-year nurse during a pandemic). Our advice saw an insurance company successfully distribute their call centre into the homes of hundreds of employees, and a retail customer to keep their entire supply chain from factory to store connected despite considerable supply pressures.

We did what felt like three years of work in just three months. Our 'work is a thing you do, not a place you go' value was being demonstrated day after day. Our customer's expectation of 'being on site' for workshops disappeared, and the amount of travel we did plummeted overnight. At the time of writing this preface, I still haven't got on a plane for work, something I did at least fortnightly before the pandemic; and can't see a need to for a while yet.

Our work was hectic, and it was rewarding. But in parallel, our team was starting to feel the strain... as our usual 'work from home' context that we were used to had changed as well. With two children doing their schoolwork from home, and my wife supporting her accounting clients away from her office, we had a real estate, internet bandwidth, and focus challenge on our hands. My wife called shotgun on the home study, and the kids switched between the small desks in their rooms, and the kitchen table regularly. I ended up in the garage, with 2 x 1m squares of commercial carpet, a dining room chair, and a blow mould plastic picnic table sourced from the local hardware shop about a week before they sold out (when large organisations came to terms with the need to distribute their workforces quickly). This impromptu office/live stream production desk worked well for a few weeks, until the other side of the garage turned into our temporary dance studio (for our girls), and gymnasium (for me) as we all engaged in 'extracurricular' activities via socially distant video.

I had to time important customer calls, workshops, and presentations with military precision, to ensure that I had wrapped up a call at 3:58pm, so that two ballerinas could do their ballet class at 4:00pm. Like many parents around the world, we just scraped through with a few tears and a handful of frustrating moments along the way.

Despite that, I know that we have been lucky in the COVID-19 lottery. We still can work. Our children can still engage in learning. We are healthy. I know that isn't the same for a large number of our community.

I think for all of us though... despite the challenges, frustration, pain, and suffering that has been caused by the pandemic, we have a great opportunity ahead of us. As organisations navigate 'surviving', and transition to 'recovering', we have an opportunity to reflect. We all just got thrown into the world's largest 'new ways of working' experiment that there has ever been. Some organisations did well, some did not. Some teams thrived, whilst others burned out. No one got it right, not even us. Now that we know that the work practices we held near and dear to our hearts may not actually help us to achieve our shared goals, over the next few years we have the chance to rethink what work is, what it means, and the way we work together. Together, we can take everything we just learned and create a workplace not for the future – but for the right now.

Which is why we decided to come together and write this book. For some, working with technologies like Microsoft 365 to improve the way that teams deliver value is nothing new. For most, they have just scratched the surface of what is possible for the first time. In many organisations, the introduction of cloud technologies like Microsoft Teams, SharePoint, and Yammer, to keep us connected as we shift to secure remote work, has been easy. For others, hard. We all have different focuses, different skillsets and different experiences. But we all have a common goal – we just want to get our work done. If we do that, we can get our lunch break back. We can get out of the 'virtual' office on time. And we can spend more time with our loved ones.

The power of a great recipe

One of the things that kept my mind off the craziness of trying to navigate a business through a pandemic, and to shut down my mind at the end of the COVID workday, was cooking for my family. Whether it was a simple Monday night meal, or a Saturday night masterpiece, the process of exploring different cuisines, unearthing new recipes, and creating new experiences took me away into another place. The ability to get different flavours and textures from different ingredients and processes... the discovery of a new herb or spice that added that something special to a meal... and the fast feedback from two 10 year old girls (generally positive, with a few 'gagging' or 'DAD, I need some water my mouth is on fire!' moments) was the escape that I needed when it felt like the world wasn't cooperating.

Cooking is the one thing that crosses all boundaries. Every culture. Every country. Every language. A great meal can bring people together and create a memorable experience for all. It is this memorable experience which is the inspiration for this book. Every home has at least one (or twenty) recipe books to help you bring your culinary aspirations to life. This recipe book is not for home. We want to help you become the executive chef at work, responsible for creating amazing experiences.

Except this time, you will not be using ingredients from the local fruit market, butcher, or bakery. Instead, we are going to take ideas and frameworks from the culinary world and apply them to our professional lives. The ingredients are different (Teams instead of Turnips, SharePoint instead of Strawberries, Yammer instead of Yams, and the Power Platform instead of Pomegranate), but the goal is still the same – crafting an experience for us and our family at work – our teammates, our department, our entire organisation.

Experiences empowered by the technology at our fingertips. The ingredients in the pantry that is Microsoft 365 – tools that make our work engaging, memorable, and better for all.

We hope you enjoy "Gourmet Teamwork", and like any recipe book, take inspiration from it to create your own recipes that result in productivity, success, and a bit more balance in our overwhelming lives.

Bon Appetit!

Paul Woods
Founder
Adopt & Embrace

… and now General Manager – Adopt & Embrace, at Rapid Circle

INTRODUCTION

*"If you are a chef, no matter how good a chef you are, it's
not good cooking for yourself; the joy is in cooking for
others - it's the same with music.*
-will.i.am

A good cook starts with an idea for a recipe, finds a
recipe they'd like to try out, then pulls together
the best ingredients and equipment needed to make a
delicious meal. However, a great cook can do all that
but also somehow add a little bit of their own magic to
make the meal extra special.

In this book, we have given you the basic recipes for
teamwork and collaboration using a variety of different
Microsoft tools you have available, however, like the
great cooks, we encourage you to also add your own
'magic herbs and spices' to make it your own. Relevant
to your needs and applications for your teams,
departments, and organisations.

The book is split into three parts.

The first part of the book focuses on the ingredients. Without these, in effect you're rendered useless. The ingredients we're using are the suite of Microsoft 365 programs that many organisations currently have access to with their enterprise licences. However, don't expect the ingredients to be hard-to-find, niche, or specialised. That is why we have focussed our recipes on the typical programs an organisation would use for their knowledge work, modern teamwork, and collaboration. We do not cover the more technical aspects of Microsoft 365.

The second part of the book focusses on the new skills your workforce may need to navigate through a changing workplace. The intention of the second chapter is to enable you to highlight those skills and areas that need to be developed in your teams, in order to use and exploit the use of the ingredients, to support your overall business goals. That is, you can have the ingredients but if you don't have the skills to pull them together in such a way to create a meal that your team may enjoy, you're missing an opportunity – as well as wasting time for you and your team – to understand how they can help you do your best work.

The third part of the book focuses on the recipes. These are the use cases where we pull together our ingredients and our skills and create our special magic.

What are we creating? We're creating custom and personalised hybrid work recipes that you can use for your own purposes. We have pulled together the use cases from different industries we have worked in, along with the typical business problems they were trying to solve and created the recipes for how they overcame their own teamwork and collaboration challenges.

All the use cases have been tried with our customers, so we're happy to share them here with you so that you can make them your own.

So, grab your aprons and let's start cooking.

PART ONE:
INGREDIENTS

"I feel a recipe is only a theme, which an intelligent cook can play each time with a variation."
– Madam Benoit

MICROSOFT 365 APPS
WORD, EXCEL, POWERPOINT

What you need to know

- Word, Excel, and PowerPoint are the foundations of knowledge work. When used well, they can help you to effectively communicate detail, transform data into meaning, and visually tell a story.
- Mastery of one of these ingredients can set you up for a rewarding career. Master all three and you will have a unique differentiator in your workplace (and the broader job market)
- Get into the habit of saving your content to the cloud (using OneDrive or SharePoint). This will enable you to easily share your work with others and allow them to collaborate with you on your document/spreadsheet/presentation without the need to email back and forward.

Learn more about this ingredient

Word, Excel and PowerPoint are the go-to applications in the Office suite most of us are familiar with. Whether it is requirements report, the project financials, or presentation pack for the Steering Committee meeting, these tools are the basis of getting work done – both individually and as a team.

Because Word, Excel, and PowerPoint have been the common fabric of knowledge work since "The Microsoft Office for Windows" was released in November 1990… we are going to assume you already understand what is possible with these tools at a high level. So, let's dive into some specifics.

With the Microsoft 365 versions of your favourite Office apps being rolled out by organisations around the world, you may notice that updates are happening a lot more frequently than the Office apps you used to know. New features may appear monthly, instead of every two years or whenever you upgraded versions. To help us make sense of the changes, you will see pop-ups appear every now and then. The pop-ups tell us when things have changed, or new functionality has been added. So next time, take a moment to read that pop-up and don't be too quick to dismiss them – it may help you know what has changed, and enable you to save some time in the future.

If you want to just recap what has changed in the past few months – click on the help tab in the ribbon menu, and you will see the What's New option. Whilst you are there, click on "Show Training" to get access to Microsoft's free online training to help you better lay out pages, work with tables, get to know Power Query, work with linked data types, or even work with 3D models in PowerPoint. This training is at your fingertips at any time within your favourite office app.

Quick Recipe:
Access free product training

1. Open up Word, Excel, or PowerPoint
2. Click on the "Help" tab in the ribbon menu
3. Click on "Show Training"
4. Browse the free online training options, and click on the skills you want to improve
5. Watch the online learning content that opens in your browser
6. Click on the "Take me there" button to see exactly where that feature or function lives within the product.

Beyond the training built into the products, don't be afraid to check out YouTube, TikTok, or Instagram Reels (depending on what generation you are from!). There are hundreds of amazing content producers creating both long form and short and sharp (in some cases just 30 seconds long) learning content that can help you level up your proficiency very quickly. Before you scoff at the potential of micro learning and Office, take a few minutes to watch some of the content from two of our favourite TikTokers:

- Mike Tholfsen - Microsoft tips (@mtholfsen)
- Kat: Chief Excel Officer (@miss.excel)

There is a tonne of information available for you to learn from, so we encourage you to keep exploring.

Today we also have access to Word, Excel, and PowerPoint wherever you are in the world, and on whatever device you are using. It could be via the web, on your iPad, or on your mobile. By saving your files to OneDrive or SharePoint, you can access your work from any of your devices. The shared "recently accessed files" list will be consistent across all those files. Perfect for quickly reviewing a presentation you developed on your desktop, or from your phone in the back of a car on the way to an important meeting.

Quick recipe:
Access your work from anywhere

1. Install Word, Excel, or PowerPoint on your mobile phone or iPad (download them from the App Store or Google Play)

2. Work on your document, spreadsheet or presentation on your regular computer or laptop
3. Save your work to OneDrive (or SharePoint)
4. Open up the relevant app on your mobile phone
5. Click on the file (it should be at the top of your recently accessed files list)
6. Review, or make minor edits whilst you are on the go

This is so powerful, especially when you might be working a few days at home, and a few days in the office (as we all seem to be in this hybrid work world today). So, while you might start the creation of your document, spreadsheet, or slideshow with the full functionality of the desktop product, for quick access you might make minor edits on a web version or even just read and review via the mobile apps. Exactly the same documents, all synced and updated with changes, and automatically version controlled.

The other thing I found when using these tools throughout my career, is that my usage of a particular product changed based on the role I was in at the time.

When I was working in the legal industry, it was all about Word. An incredibly powerful tool to create and manage often huge documents and I have to say we often pushed it to its limit. It is certainly where I learnt all my tips and tricks. You just don't have time to do things the hard way in law, things were changing too fast; but they were also sticklers for efficiencies and consistency. This is where Word bought it home. Using templates that used functionality like cover pages, headers/footers, and styles, provided the opportunity to create documents that had a consistent look and feel, irrelevant of who created them.

When it came to mark ups, lawyers do it best. Every change was marked up, every addition and deletion redlined, so it was clear which changes had been made and commentary that was required to support the change. Comparing and reviewing documents was part of the day-to-day workings.

Quick Recipe:
View and Compare two documents side by side

1. Open up both the documents you want to compare
2. Click on the "View" tab
3. Click on "View Side by Side"
4. To scroll both documents at the same time, click on "Syncronous Scrolling".

Let's not forget the old mail merge, thankfully not something I have to do a lot of these days but something that is still incredibly powerful and faster than typing out hundreds of letters to clients individually. Yikes.

I also use it to whip up the company newsletter or the social club flyer and with borders and graphics options, made it look professional and polished.

Even this book was created in Word, providing us the functionality, durability, and professional touches, like bookmarking, table of contents, cross-referencing, and bibliography.

When I shifted away from Law and into Finance, Excel became my go-to tool. At first it was a little daunting as I'd never needed to use it before. The thing about Excel is, you have to have a reason. It is an incredibly powerful tool, if you know how to use it but more importantly, if you need to use it. You could debate the performance difference between a vLookup and Index Match, but surely you have better things to do with your life. So, while I was no financial analyst, those who were, got all they needed from Excel formulae and could create financial models to support almost any situation or transaction.

Personally, I was more of a list person. I used Excel to list, filter, and keep track across projects I was working on. I loved a good pivot table to slice and dice data, and in fact, still do. I was lucky enough to be taught an easy way to use pivot tables and they don't scare me at all now. In fact, those people I have shown can't believe they have been afraid of them in the past. With a bit of conditional formatting, I was able to see changes quickly and identify patterns in my work.

Quick Recipe:
Create a Pivot Table

1. Enter your data into Excel

2. Make sure you have column headings
3. Select your data
4. Click on the "Insert" tab in the ribbon
5. Click on "PivotTable"
6. Click "ok"
7. On the new worksheet that appears, experiment with selecting and filtering to help you make meaning of your data.

These days I am probably spending more time in PowerPoint than I have ever done before. When you need your work to be more about a graphical representation to tell a story rather than people having to read endless words, then PowerPoint is the tool for you.

Whilst you can make things morph, fly, or transform, it can be just as powerful with a less is more approach.

Even our reports are done in PowerPoint these days. We can say so much more with a chart or image than we could with lots of words. We tell the story.

We also have the opportunity of humanising our work, when people see imagery that reflects them or their industry it is an easier message to get across. We have the opportunity of providing consistency and efficiencies with templates, masters, and design ideas.

It doesn't matter what product you are using to create. You start with an idea and build on it. In this digital world, we have the opportunity of updating, changing, and enhancing our ideas and getting feedback and input from others.

Now that our documents are saved to online spaces, we don't even have to have multiple copies of documents – hallelujah. We can call in a member of our team with a simple @mention in the comments and ask for their advice or input. Document review and or approvals have never been so easy, and we can provide links to a single document, with automatic version control. We don't even need to know how to spell or write correctly, as it will tell us where we can do better along the way. How good is that? It is like having your own master chef beside you.

Quick Recipe:
Gather feedback on your file

1. Create your masterpiece in Word, Excel, or PowerPoint
2. Save the file to OneDrive (or SharePoint)
3. Press the "Share" button in the top right-hand corner, and invite your reviewers into the document
4. Encourage them to add comments to the file (using the "New Comment" button which you can find in the "Review" tab)
5. When responding to comments your reviewers make, @mention their name to get their attention. This will send them a notification that you are

asking for more advice or have taken their feedback on board.

Word, Excel, and PowerPoint also seamlessly integrate into Microsoft Teams. When we are working in Microsoft Teams, we can link our created documents to our posts irrelevant of where they are stored, and our team members will have the access they need. So, we have all the tools we need, in the spaces we need, so our people can access what they need.

So again, it goes to show that you use what you need to use. You don't have to use everything, but it helps to keep up with the updates and changes, read them, understand them, know if they can help you make your life easier, and then put them into practice. Also, don't forget to share with your colleagues as well. There are plenty of sites where you can learn more tips and tricks about these products, so when you learn something new, share it with someone else.

We don't know what we don't know.

Get Cooking with Word, Excel, or PowerPoint:

1. Learn more about the Office Suite via the https://support.microsoft.com/en-au/office
2. Download the apps to your desktop and devices
3. Open your menus and check out what functionality is available

4. Save documents in cloud-based storage to take advantage of version control
5. Set a goal to learn a new tip each week and share it with a colleague
6. Access printable graphics, quick start guides and office cheat sheets at:

   https://support.microsoft.com/en-us/office/great-ways-to-work-with-office-6fe70269-b9a4-4ef0-a96e-7a5858b3bd5a
7. Keep up to date with What's New at:

   https://support.microsoft.com/en-us/topic/what-s-new-in-microsoft-365-95c8d81d-08ba-42c1-914f-bca4603e1426?wt.mc_id=otc_office_basics&ui=en-us&rs=en-us&ad=us

ONENOTE

What you need to know

- OneNote may not be as well-known as Word or Outlook, but is an equal, if not more valuable ingredient in your workday
- OneNote is used to replace (or complement) your paper-based notebooks, with additional capability that your paper-based notebook can't provide (like taking photos and putting them in the context of your notes, search to instantly find the notes you are looking for, or converting your handwriting into text)

- OneNote is great for taking notes in meetings, creating lists, capturing ideas, mind mapping, and organising your thoughts.

Learn more about this ingredient

Ever been to the doctor, and whilst waiting, you read the magazine in the corner and found a recipe that you like? Well, in the days before mobiles, some people would tear out the recipe and took it home. Now we can be a little more civilised and take a photo, leaving the magazine intact for others. 'I must find where I saved the photo or remember when I took it… hmmm, maybe I need to be a little more organised?'

I recently found my mum's recipe book that had her beautiful handwritten recipes, potentially shared with or from her mother and sisters. The edges were torn and tattered, not to mention, stained with an assortment of ingredients from the past.

But I also found a heap of cut out recipes that had been captured over the years.

The beauty of a notebook is it allows us to capture not only the recipe, but our thoughts of it. Our additions or subtractions that made it our own.

But the problem about a notebook, is that it does run out of room, becomes faded, tattered and worn out, or contains so many extra sheets that carrying it around may be a hazard not only to ourselves but to others as well.

I have always been a keen notetaker in my personal and work life, and still have a selection of notebooks from past roles capturing, what at the time was a wealth of information. But the problem was when I really needed it, I had to remember which notebook it was in, and then flick, what seemed like endlessly, to find what I was looking for, only to be more often disappointed and giving up without getting what I needed.

I was introduced to OneNote Notebooks some time ago. In fact, they all laughed at me when I continued to write in my notebooks, saying it was my preferred way. But over time I was converted and have to say, never looked back.

I can do so much more with my digital notebook than I could ever do with a physical notebook. Not only can I capture notes, but I can take photos, record audio and video, insert files, print outs and images. I can organise it, move things around, add or delete anywhere. In fact, OneNote is now a part of my day-to-day life.

I am not limited to a size or number of pages nor everything having to be in one notebook.

I can keep personal or private notebooks for different information, and I can create and share notebooks with others.

Before COVID, I would use it for travel. For larger holidays I would create a separate notebook and plan and identify places I wanted to go, things I wanted to see, and events I wanted to attend. As I would move into the booking stages, I would capture confirmations, tickets, and event details as well as itineraries, accommodation, and flight details. Whilst I was travelling, I would use it as a travel diary, capturing not only photos, but details about the places, experiences, thoughts, and details of people I had met along the way. I also have a smaller holiday notebook and I could create a new section for each place.

Another advantage is that I don't need to be carting a laptop around to do this. I can access OneNote across all my devices, and it will automatically sync. So, while I might plan on the laptop, I could be sitting in the taxi, providing the address of my hotel from the itinerary printed in my OneNote on my phone. I can then take a photo on my phone and save it straight to OneNote whilst out and about, and when I get back to the hotel, I can add all my thoughts and experiences via my tablet. I could even share the notebook with my family and friends so they could keep up to date with my travel experiences live.

I have used it to capture all those old recipes of my mother. Taking photos of her handwritten recipes, preserving them for ever but also giving me to the opportunity to add my own flavour to those recipes, my additions, thoughts, or memories of eating some of those dishes. One of my favourite features of OneNote is that it has built in search... and search works on all that content I save to my digital notebook – including the handwritten notes that I took photos of!

Quick Recipe:
Search for notes in OneNote

1. Capture your text, handwritten notes (using a stylus), pictures, documents, printouts, snippets, audio and video recordings etc in your OneNote notebook
2. Click on the search box in the top right-hand corner of the screen
3. Start typing your search term
4. Watch as the different pages across all of your notebooks start to filter. Click on the appropriate page
5. Look on the page, and your search term will be highlighted (including the handwriting on your mother's recipe).

Once I had captured the recipes, I then shared that OneNote notebook with other family members. I have to say that I only gave them read rights, so they could experience the knowledge shared by my mother, but I kept control of the family recipes. They could still submit their entries or thoughts and I would add them to the notebook for others to see.

I have found real value using these digital notebooks for teamwork. Information that needed to be shared previously was often emailed around, whether you wanted it or not. When you create a Microsoft Team, a OneNote Notebook is automatically created and is easily added as a tab for everyone to access. You can even add different sections to different channels so you can keep organised.

So now when a team member takes notes at a meeting, instead of them being captured in a Word document and then emailed, they can be captured directly into the Team OneNote Notebook, and everyone can access to those shared notes. You can copy links to sections, pages or paragraphs and add the links to conversations posts to let others know about the meetings. It even integrates with Outlook, picking up the meeting details from the invitation, including the name of the meeting, the date and time, and even the participants names: all the things we start to capture as soon as we get in the meeting, so it has already saved us some time. After the meeting, if we need to, we can email the notes to those who are outside our team.

Quick Recipe:
Add the meeting details to your OneNote notes

1. Create a new page in the relevant section of your OneNote Notebook

2. Click on the "Meeting Details" button (it is on the "Home" tab, at the far-right hand side)
3. Click on the relevant meeting based on the information drawn from your Outlook calendar
4. Watch as OneNote adds a title to your page (the subject of the meeting), the details of the meeting (date, time, location), and the participants of the meeting
5. Tick the attendance box beside each attendee as they join the meeting
6. Take your notes on the rest of the page as the meeting progresses
7. Click "Email Page" (just to the left of the "Meeting Details" button) to share the meeting notes with others via email at the end of the meeting.

We have also used OneNote to capture emails. When an email is sent to an individual, it can be locked or trapped in a personal, non-accessible place, but when printed to OneNote, everyone can see the email and notes can be added as to what action is required or has been taken. You can also print reference material, or pre-meeting reading material, instead of sending attachments around. Everyone can access the same information, add their own notes and others can see everything in one place.

Quick Recipe:
Print a document to OneNote

1. Open up your document, spreadsheet, PDF, or web page
2. Click on "Print"
3. Select "Print to OneNote" from the printer selection box
4. Click "Print"
5. Select the notebook/section or page where you want the printout to be placed
6. Go to that page in OneNote and start adding your notes or markup.

You can also have your to do list in OneNote. In fact, you can tag a whole range of important information across the notebook, not having to worry where it was written because the find tags feature will bring them all together into one place and hyperlink each entry, making it easy to find.

Where once we might have created Word documents to capture project notes, we now capture it all in one place, together as a team, that we can all stay on the same page and using conversations we can link off to the more detail as we need it. You can even use OneNote for dictation. So, if you don't want to write or type, you can still get those creative juices flowing, and it will capture as you speak.

Do you see that I am a fan? Yes, it is true. I have been converted to digital notetaking. OneNote would have to be one of my favourite applications and used daily. I have not carried a notebook for a long time, nor have I printed anything in years. It all gets printed to OneNote, so I am also doing my bit for the environment as well.

Be aware that there are two versions of OneNote. The free version that comes with Windows called OneNote for Windows 10, and OneNote (previously called OneNote 2016) which comes with your Office 365 subscription.

There are some functionality differences but overall, both applications will make your life much easier than a physical notebook. You will be able to tell the difference because OneNote has more functionality (more menus) than OneNote for Windows 10.

Now when I see that recipe in the surgery waiting room, I can just take a photo and post it straight into my recipe notebook, and when I am at the shops, I can see all the ingredients I need from my phone and have all the details on how to make it when I get home. A win-win for me.

Get Cooking with OneNote:

1. Learn more about OneNote
   https://support.microsoft.com/en-us/office/video-what-is-onenote-be6cc6cc-3ca7-4f46-8876-5000f013c563

2. Download the app to your desktop and devices
3. Start small, capture some notes, organise yourself with some sections and add some pages
4. Use the search function to find a word or phrase
5. Take your meetings to the next level, by adding meeting details from the OneNote Home Ribbon
6. Print team information to a centralised Team Notebook and add a link to the conversation
7. Consider creating Notebooks for both personal and work. Create your own Recipe or Travel book
8. Read how others are using OneNote
   https://www.microsoft.com/en-us/microsoft-365/blog/onenote/

SHAREPOINT & ONEDRIVE

What you need to know

- Saving your files to the cloud in SharePoint or OneDrive gives you advantages over saving them locally – like automatic version history, the ability to work on the file with others, and reduced risk of losing your work
- OneDrive is private to you by default, and is great for working drafts before you share them more broadly
- Files in SharePoint are generally visible to more people in your organisation, and is great for working on content with others or making your work more discoverable
- SharePoint is the file storage that sits behind Microsoft Teams – so if you are working with files in Teams, you are really using SharePoint in disguise

- SharePoint also has other organisation wide or team specific use cases, like the ability to create an intranet, or project-based site.

Learn more about this ingredient

Creating stuff is at the essence of what we do, but creating is only part of it. I need to put it somewhere. I then need to be able to find it again. Sometimes I need others to find it as well or even work on it with me. We might need to work together to make it perfect.

So, I need a safe and secure place to save my work and there is none safer than OneDrive or SharePoint. I must admit, I don't miss shared network drives. S:\ drive, M:\ drive, T:\ drive. Yuck. My life is so much easier working in the cloud. The fact that I can work from anywhere is one of the many benefits, which was particularly helpful during a global pandemic, but that is certainly not the only benefit.

There are some people out there who may have some concerns about information being stored in the cloud, but as I see it, every text, call or social media interaction I have is in the cloud anyway, and the convenience far out ways the risk. Particularly when Microsoft have invested a lot more than our business could ever do in security and resilient infrastructure. Now that is not to say you shouldn't be vigilant and careful about what you are adding to the cloud and who has access to it but that is a whole other conversation. There have always been risks.

In the past, my documents were stored often on local drives, C:/ drives and USBs which caused problems when the computer had one of its many moments and decided it was at end of its life. Or, the USB failed at the critical moment on a client site when I needed to do an important presentation.

It was no better in fact when I was using the network home drives or H: drives. Whilst my documents were not as reliant on failing hardware, if I was away from the office, I had to default to other hardware or access the documents via VPN and I have to say, my experience with that software was not always kind.

Now I turn on my computer and I have access to all my personal files and those shared with my colleagues. I can even access them when I am offline. Even better, it doesn't have to be my computer. I can access those same files via any device, including my desktop computer at the office, my laptop when working from home, my iPad when reading a file after work with a glass of wine on the back deck, or on my mobile device to get information on the go. I simply save the document to my secure, compliant cloud-based office 365 tool OneDrive for Business or SharePoint Online and I can work anywhere I need to.

So, what is the difference between saving documents to OneDrive for Business and SharePoint Online?

Well OneDrive is my personal space. When I save documents to OneDrive, they are by default private. No one else can access them unless I choose to give them access.

I can create my own files and folders and access them wherever I go. I will often use OneDrive as my starting point, where I will do my brain dump and massage it into some sort of readable order and then, I can provide share links to documents if I need input or collaboration with others and stop sharing whenever I want. I have full control.

I also like that there is only one copy of the document. With automatic version control, I can revert to earlier versions if someone has made changes to a document that I am not happy with, and I don't ever have to worry if I am using the latest document, as there is only one document - ever.

Quick recipe:
Go back to a previous version

1. Create your work in Word, Excel, or PowerPoint
2. Save it to OneDrive or SharePoint
3. Continue to work on your file

4. Realise you made a big mistake earlier today, and you want to go back and look at your previous version of the file
5. Look to the top of your screen, and look for where the file name of your document/spreadsheet/presentation is
6. Click on the little arrow that is just to the right-hand side of the file name
7. Click on "Version History" on the pop-up menu that appears
8. Select the version of the file you want to review and/or restore.

Some of us like 'how we have always done things'. If you are a fan of File Explorer, you can sync your files from OneDrive to File Explorer for a more familiar experience, should you wish to navigate like days of yore. But I don't even need to do that anymore. As the documents are stored in the cloud, I can use the Windows Search function at the desktop level, type in a word or phase of the document name or content, and it would find the document for me, irrelevant if I had 35 folders or not. It is like "having people" to do things for you. So why would you do it yourself?

So, OneDrive for Business, is secure, compliant, personal by default, provides multiple share options should I need them, lets me work from anywhere on any device, creating a single file with automatic version control.

So, what is SharePoint Online then? And how is it different to "SharePoint"?

Well let's start there; the old SharePoint that people refer to were often "on prem" or on premises. Think of it like big filing cabinets that were managed by the IT departments. They determined who had access to what cabinets and getting that changed or updated was sometimes a battle. Access to those filing cabinets were restricted by membership permissions that again needed to be managed by IT or SharePoint administrators.

SharePoint was often used as a document repository only, however if set up well, it had some powerful functionality to connect information and people together.

I think it has been made easier with SharePoint Online, as the interface is much easier to navigate and creation of SharePoint pages and webparts no longer requires administrator rights or capability. You can create Communication Sites, or they can be linked to Microsoft Teams (Team Sites). Team Sites are still often used predominately as document repositories via the files tab of Teams. So, when you click on the Files tab in Teams, you are accessing the associated SharePoint online document library and every time you create a channel in a Team, you are creating a folder in that document library to store the associated channel files.

Like OneDrive, documents stored in SharePoint Online, are cloud based, automatically version controlled but the benefit over OneDrive is that it is automatically shared with everyone who is a member of the Team. I don't have to physically type in every single person's name as I would in the share link of OneDrive. Adding a document to a channel in a Team, means that everyone in the Team can access and edit it, whether they need to or not and, because of the version history, if they "muck it up", no issue, I can restore it to a previous version.

I can also easily share the file from the Teams file tab to someone outside the Team and based on my organisational settings, this could be internally to another department or externally to a supplier or vendor. They don't get access to everything in the Team, just the file that I have shared.

Communication sites are a bit different, often used and created as intranets or project micro sites, they are more graphical in design opportunities. You can add or remove a variety of different types of webparts on either a Team Site or Communication site to suit your needs. You can still create document libraries in a communication site that is not linked to a Team.

Often corporate departments have their own communication site or pages within a communicate site, particularly cross group departments like HR, WHS, Finance, or Marketing as they are often the ones providing corporate documents like policies, or templates, or procedures. It might also be a space where people can catch up on corporate news and events and just like the name, it is all about corporate wide communications.

But again, the biggest advantage of SharePoint Online is that I can access it from anywhere, without a VPN. I can access documents from team sites or from the associated SharePoint Library. I can search and filter for documents across the site and add loads of meta data (key information) to bring information together in manageable blocks. I can access from any device including my desktop or mobile devices and I can still sync it to File Explorer for that familiar experience or access it from the online sites.

So, think of it this way:

- **OneDrive** for **Me** (Personal and private)
- **SharePoint Teams Sites** for **We** (members of my Team)
- **SharePoint Communication Sites** for **Us** (Organisation wide)

Now this sounds to me like a recipe for success.

Get Cooking with OneDrive and SharePoint:

1. Learn more about OneDrive and SharePoint https://support.microsoft.com/en-au/onedrive?ui=en-us&rs=en-au&ad=au

2. Download the apps to your desktop and devices
3. Sync your OneDrive for Business & SharePoint document libraries to File Explorer
4. Clean up that C:\drive or desktop and move all those USB sticks to your OneDrive and get your files in the cloud where they will be safe and secure
5. Navigate to the associated files tab of a Team Site to access the SharePoint Online functionality
6. Upload your latest files from Network Drives to your team sites and connect them to conversations so people
7. Watch the SharePoint Training video at: https://support.microsoft.com/en-us/office/sharepoint-video-training-cb8ef501-84db-4427-ac77-ec2009fb8e23

MICROSOFT TEAMS

What you need to know

- Teams is more than just chat messages and video conferencing
- When used well, it can reduce your reliance on email and meetings
- The "Superpower" of Teams is to connect people, content, and processes, all within the context of your work.

Learn more about this ingredient

I don't know if Microsoft Teams is the ingredient or the pot that mixes everything together. I know I can make wonderful recipes within Teams to create amazing opportunities to communicate, collaborate, and coordinate tasks and events. So maybe it is the Thermomix of pots?

But like most things, it can take a while to get the recipe right.

I know when we first started using Teams, all the "young" ones where straight onto it, trying this and trying that. I was a bit slower to the table, testing, and tasting, trying a little bit here and a little bit there, until I finally got a taste for it.

And now... I couldn't think of a life without it.

I love that I have choices. I can work where I want to work, and if that is all in Teams, it works best for me, as it minimises the switching cost.

I can chat with my colleagues one-to-one or in small groups, without having to jump out to another product and convert those chats to audio and video calls. I know when I have missed a chat as it is bolded and provides with a badge like texts on my phone. I also love that those chats and calls are integrated with Outlook, so I can respond with instant messaging or calls directly from an email. There is a complete conversation history in Outlook as well, so if I wasn't sure where the conversation took place, I can search, and it will find it for me.

I can join my meetings from Teams. No longer having to leave what I am working on, open Outlook, open calendar, open the invitation, click the link, tell it to use my desktop app so I can join the meeting... I get exhausted just thinking about it. Now all I do is click on the Calendar app on the side navigation bar, it shows me everything I have on for the day and if it is a Teams meeting, it says Join, so I just click on that. I can also create all my meetings that I need directly from the

Calendar app – in fact, it is virtually the same as my Outlook Calendar.

But the Teams App is where the real magic happens.

Where I can work with the people I need to work with and get done whatever needs to get done. I can have different Teams for different people or different types of work. I can give the focus to the teams that need it the most at any point in time, and even when we are working in different phases or roles within a team, we can have our own space or channel to have those focused conversations or share those files and it is not all dumped into one space.

I remember trying to communicate with team members when working on multiple priorities or projects at one time using Outlook. Trying to curate conversations that changed mid-stream and then finding all those conversations again if my filing was not up to date or asking myself if I filed it in the right place? Now I go to the Team that I am working on with all those people and I can see a complete history of everything we have done. All the decisions and how we go there all available in one space. I think of all the times I joined a team mid-stream and was sent hundreds of emails to "get up to speed". Now I can go to the beginning of the channel and read the threads of conversation and see how decisions were made.

The real beauty is that with email, I had to be sure I had everyone that was relevant on the email address, which meant often, people were getting CC'd where they didn't need to know anything at all, it was all in case or for situational awareness. Now because I am a member of a Team, I can go to any channel and see what is going on if I have time or inclination to do so. I can see what others are doing, and if it is going to impact me, I can and my commentary and everyone can see it.

I can see what I have read and what I haven't read, so can choose my priorities and action the items that need my immediate attention and catch up later with the less important conversations. I can filter by activity so I can return to a previous conversation easily even if I don't remember exactly where it was.

When it comes to files? Wow, the effort we all put into collaborating with files in emails. It makes me cringe just thinking of the wasted time and effort when we attach a file. There are multiple copies of the document on drives, sent folders and inboxes, no one knows which copy of a document anyone is working on and everyone saves their version with their initials, so we end up with version 1, version 1.1, version 1.1.1. Bobs edits, version 1.1.1.1.1 Final, version 1.1.1.1.1 Final, version 1.1.1.1.1 Final really use this one final… and you get my drift.

Now, every time you create a channel, it automatically provides you with a dedicated Files repository, managed by SharePoint Online in the backend, with all the functionality and security.

Everyone who is a member of the Team, can access the files, edit the files, and create new files and there is automatic version control and even IF someone makes changes to your Word document without your knowledge, you can compare and mark up your document based on the previous version.

I can remember the days when I was working in document control, and I would send out a document for review to up to 20 people and I would get back 20 copies of the document that I had to compare and combine. Now I send out a sharing link, even if the people are not in my Team and they can access that document, make their edits and suggestions. All in one document. I can then make the required updates and send a sharing link to the approvers. So much easier and saving so much time.

If you are still fixated by folders, you can create those as well, but I don't know about you, but I have spent too long navigating rabbit warrens of folder structures only to find out that someone else's "logic" wasn't so logical for me. I much prefer to search for what I am looking for. Like to the old advert for the Yellow Pages used to say here in Australia, "Let my fingers to the walking". I can search for conversations, files, or people. I can add filters for types of documents or date ranges or even from certain teams and believe me – the system can find it much fast than I can. The search is so powerful, it can search for file names and document content, so it is hard not to find what you are looking for.

I can even create documents, using any of the office tools, directly from the Teams environment. Whilst it might initially create or view them in Teams, I can choose to continue to work in the online versions or use the desktop versions if I prefer. The choice is always mine, based on what I need to do, what functionality I need, or where I prefer to work.

Collaboration is a breeze now. I can link those conversations to files, providing context about how or why the file was created and don't forget about that history. Even if someone finds it much later, they will know why. Instead of a folder that was created by a team member that you don't know why or what any of the files were used for.

So, every channel has its own place to have conversations and a place to store files – but these are not the only tools we use in a day – which is where Tabs come in. At the top of every channel, you can add the tabs to the tools your channel needs. You can add OneNote notebooks to capture shared information like emails, meeting notes or research material. You can add a Team Planner to coordinate tasks and assign them to the members of the team. You can add links to external websites or tools like Jira or Asana, providing you with access to all the tools you need in one convenient space.

Quick recipe:
Add a visual planning or task board to your channel

1. Select the relevant channel in your team
2. Click on the "+" button beside the tabs at the top of your screen
3. Select "Planner" or "Tasks by Planner and ToDo" from the "Add a tab" pop up that appears
4. Start adding columns to your board to categorise your work, and cards for each action item
5. Check out the Planner chapter later in this part of the book to dive deeper into how to get the most out of your task board.

Teams is a hub for Teamwork. A place to get work done, with the people you need to work with. Focusing files and conversations in a curated organised way but integrated with all the other Office 365 tools that you could possibly need. A place where recipes for Teamwork come to life.

Get Cooking with Microsoft Teams:

1. Learn more at: https://support.microsoft.com/en-au/teams.
2. Download the apps to your desktop and devices
3. Dive deeper into Teams. Read our earlier book – Adopt & Embrace Microsoft Teams: A Manager's Guide to Communication, Collaboration and Co-

ordination https://teamsbook.info/ or search for it on Amazon

4. Consider the 10P framework when creating teams. You can download the framework in the Resources section at: https://teamsbook.info/

5. Onboard your team members and work together to plan the recipe for success.

TEAMS WEBINARS AND LIVE EVENTS

What you need to know

- You can use Microsoft Teams to deliver public (or private) virtual events. Like all-hands meetings, company updates, or marketing events
- Webinars are an easy way to deliver interactive meeting experiences, with a registration gate to capture attendee details
- Live Events allow you to deliver large events at scale in a more polished, controlled way.

Learn more about this ingredient

During the pandemic many of us have become more familiar with the video call, or video meeting. They are a great way to connect and engage with our colleague 1:1, or in small groups. But what if you need to scale your influence beyond your manager, direct report, or your project team? This is where the webinar and live event capability in Microsoft Teams can help.

Think of webinars and live events as different varieties of the same ingredient – a Teams meeting. Much like different varieties of apples can have different colours, textures, and flavours, within Microsoft Teams we have three different flavours of video-based meeting options.

First, is the standard meeting. You can schedule it via Outlook, kick off a meeting in a Teams Channel, or "Meet Now". A quick and easy way to connect with your peers. Your participants can turn the camera on or off, they can mute themselves when not participating in the conversation, they can share their screen, and engage in the meeting chat. If you have had a meeting in Microsoft Teams, this is the meeting you would have had.

Second, is the Microsoft Teams webinar. Technically a Teams webinar is very similar to a standard Teams meeting, with a few minor exceptions. You can create an event registration page, allowing you to capture details of attendees as they register for the meeting. This makes it great for when you want to invite external stakeholders to a marketing event, or customer roundtable.

Webinars also reinforce the role of "presenters" and "attendees" giving you more fine-grained control over the meeting experience. For example, you can block the ability for attendees to turn their camera on or come off mute – until you want them to engage in the conversation.

Your Marketing team will have an interest in exploring the webinar functionality in Microsoft Teams. However, any team in an organisation could get value from this feature, particularly if you need to track registrations for an internal call or event or want to present a polished meeting with more control.

Finally, we have the Live Event. A Microsoft Teams Live Event gives you the ability to professionally produce and broadcast an event for large audiences, with moderated Q&A. Even 10 years ago, to be able to broadcast your all hands meeting, or annual general meeting, or large-scale conference presentation was a mammoth exercise. Now, not so much. The technology is relatively straight forward – from a presenter's point of view it can be as simple as joining a Teams meeting! As a producer, you just select the camera you want to go live, or the slides you want to share, and send them live to the broadcast. However, to produce a great live event, it does take some planning.

Like any large event, you probably have someone who is organising everything for you – coordinating the presenters, presentations, meeting invitations, and just generally setting everything up for you to make sure the event is a success. You may also have multiple presenters, who are coming and going throughout the session, and they are subject matter experts. However, they need to know the order of things, when they need to be in place, when they will go live, when they will start talking, how long they will talk for, who will move through the presentation at the right time. This will largely be based on what we call a cue sheet.

The Cue Sheet will detail each component of the event. The start and duration, a clear description, if there as a change in camera or audio, what content is being displayed and any notes.

A Cue Sheet is generally developed by the Producer who can be the same person as the organiser but is best suited to someone who has some experience in this area.

The producer role is probably one of the most important, as they will be the ones who line everyone up, they determine what the audience will see at any point in time and are largely responsible for the success of the event. They are also the ones that can make your event interesting or dull, by using a variety of sources that ensure each presenter and their material is shown in the best light.

In fact, in large or complex meetings, there may be multiple producers accountable for multiple roles.

- A show caller can direct the event, ensuring everyone knows what is coming next and are prepared for their role

- A Primary Switcher can be responsible for switching between different video, audio, and content sources
- A back up switcher is also a good idea with a backup device on a different network in case of a network connectivity or device issue on the day
- You can also have multiple "producers" filling the role of moderators
- Primary Q&A moderator can be responsible for managing the question time, opening, and closing the Q&A session and publishing the public responses to questions
- A secondary Q&A moderator could be responsible for private replies to Q&A participants
- And you could even have a Quality monitor, who is responsible for monitoring the live feed for video and audio quality.

It is also advisable to have some people in the background for larger and more complex events that may not be part of the show. IT Support, Network administrators and security specialists should all be available to ensure the successful event.

And again, for larger and more complex events, it may be worthwhile having a project manager to bring it all together.

For smaller live events, your organiser, producer, and moderator can be the same person.

When the event is first scheduled, these roles can be assigned, by the organiser. It is at this point that you will determine if the event is internal, like a dedicated group, a town hall style, or if it is a public event. You will also determine the live event settings, like enabling captions, recordings, and even the language translations.

By default, if it is within the organisation or private event, participants will need to sign in to gain access, however if the event is Public, by default, there is no sign in required.

Quick Recipe:
Schedule a Live Event

1. From the Calendar app in Teams
2. Use the New Meeting drop down menu in the top right corner
3. Choose Live Event
4. Add the meeting details, like title, date, time
5. Invite your Event group team including your presenters and assign their roles
6. Set the meeting permissions and production settings
7. And send it to the team.

The last and most important role that needs to be considered when running a Live Event is the audience, a role that is necessary for an event to even happen.

You can create another meeting invitation for your audience members and provide them with an attendee link. You can copy this link by clicking on the Get Attendee Link once the Live Event has been scheduled, or you can access it by using the edit function of the meeting

Once the Live Event meeting has been organised and scheduled, we would highly recommend a test run or dress rehearsal. Even if it is for a small event, schedule another session, so everyone can run through the setup, know the flow of the meeting, and iron out any issues before the big event. Set up a separate live event for your dress rehearsal, as you can't 'reuse' a scheduled live event for multiple run throughs.

And the larger the event, the more rehearsals would be recommended. I know if can be difficult to get people together, but the result will be well worth the investment in time and attention to detail.

During the rehearsals, the producer can explore the flow of the meeting, work out the best queues and displays, and when different components will go live. It is also important to note here that there is a slight time delay between what the producer is sending and what the audience is seeing.

Have some friendlies join the rehearsal sessions as audience members from external email accounts and internal accounts, from the web, tablets, and phones, and provide a forum to collate feedback and review the process.

The producer/s should be directing the presenters, checking audio, checking backgrounds, and taking notes from them as to the best displays. The moderators could also practice the Q&A environment, when to open and close question time, and determine how they will be presented to the presenters.

Quick Recipe
Create a Cue Sheet using a word document

1. Identify the role that each team member plays
2. Identify what each team member is accountable for
3. Collect contact details in the event of an emergency in the lead up to, or during the broadcast
4. Map out the flow of the event, detailing each significant moment of the event (for example, broadcast start and end times, speaker timing, when slides need to be visible on screen etc).

When all the testing has been done, the cue sheets are produced, and everyone is aligned, you are ready for the big event.

Once the event has started, there is no going back. If someone presses 'End', the show is over. Hence the practice sessions are really important.

Once your event is over, a reflection is always worthwhile. Get feedback from all the participants – your project group, organisers, producers, presenters, and moderators. What went well, what didn't go so well, and what would you change in the future.

Get feedback from your audience as well. Was the event marketed correctly? Did they have enough information on how, when, and why the event was taking place? Where the invitations sent in a timely manner? Was the attendee list correct? Did the event hit the mark for them? Did it meet their expectations? How would they improve the session?

Continual learning and reflection will ensure our continual growth.

Get Cooking with Microsoft Teams:

1. Learn more at:
   Get started with Microsoft Teams live events
2. Access the FAQ quick guide Live events FAQ (microsoft.com)
3. Get a small group together an organise a live event
4. Create a Cue Sheet for your event
5. Practice a live Event for your next team meeting
6. Create a Live Event for your next town hall.

YAMMER

What you need to know

- In many organisations, Yammer is considered their "culture platform", where people come together around shared interests, topics, or values (vs Teams where "they do their focused work")
- In a world where we can't connect in a lunchroom or around a water cooler (because many of us are working from home, or only doing a few days in the office), Yammer creates a space where your broader organisation be part of a digital community
- Being active and visible in Yammer helps create connection, and build trust across teams, departments, and organisations – a valuable ingredient in improving employee experience.

Learn more about this ingredient

Often mistakenly referred to as 'Facebook for Business', Yammer came into the scene in 2008 as an enterprise collaborative platform. Bought by Microsoft four years later, it is now part of the Microsoft 365 suite and available for businesses to use as part of their enterprise plans.

Yammer is all about building communities across your organisation. It allows employees to be able to share knowledge and connect with their peers around shared interests, purpose, values, hobbies, and more. For example, a "CEO connection" community where your workforce can engage with your leadership team about issues that matter. A "Excel Tips & Tricks" community to connect the spreadsheet warriors from across your organisation in place. Or a "Green Team" community focused on activities, behaviours, and initiatives that help reduce your organisation's negative impact on the environment.

The communities do not need to be work related either – this is especially important if we recognise that trust (an important element in the workplace) can be built through non-work conversations. "The Dogs (or Cats) of <Organisation Name>", "Cycling Central", and "Wordle Chat" all have a role to play in helping to improve employee engagement

There are a variety of ways that Yammer enables communication to happen across the organisation, which is different and unique to how Microsoft Teams is used. Where Teams is used specifically for work team collaboration and project execution, Yammer encompasses conversations that can span across work projects and may not be driven by time or client constraints. Instead, it focuses on wider knowledge sharing and storytelling approaches that cater for discovery and community engagement. These are sometimes known as 'outer loop' conversations, conversations that may occur between teams and departments (vs 'inner loop' conversations that will happen within your team, or with people you regularly work with).

As such Yammer is used in different ways, everything from leadership communication, announcing and broadcasting messages and announcements, building communities of practice or interest groups that support your employees to learn from and with each other, as well as create an environment for ideas to be developed or brainstormed. It allows for everyone in your organisation to have a voice and to converse or work together across silos. Companies have used Yammer for employee onboarding, crisis communication, running their Town Hall events and so much more.

In the previous chapter we discussed Live Events. You can produce a live event in Microsoft Teams, and have it broadcast via a Yammer community. Your internal audience watch the stream just as if it was being streamed on YouTube and can comment and react in real time, or tune in later and watch the replay.

In the context of your internal communications efforts, this allows you to create a space where your people can engage before, during, and after the event (not just whilst the broadcast is live). A simple difference, but a meaningful one when you are building a multi-channel engagement strategy.

Quick recipe:
Create a Yammer Community

1. Log into the Office 365 portal at https://portal.office.com
2. If Yammer is enabled in your organisation, switch to Yammer using the app switcher
3. Browse the communities that already exist, and join if interested in the topic
4. To create your own community (say "Pets of <organisation name>"), click on "Create a Community". If you can't see it on the bottom left-hand side of your screen, try clicking on "View All" first
5. Follow the instructions in the dialog boxes – make sure it is a public community if you want others in your organisation to discover it.

Yammer enables your people to communicate, collaborate and create together across the organisation and does so openly and inclusively. If you want to enable your people to work and connect across organisational boundaries and silos, then Yammer is the platform to explore.

Get Cooking with Yammer:

1. Read more about Yammer, download and read the Yammer Look Book
   https://teamworktools.azurewebsites.net/yammer/Yammer%20Lookbook.pdf
2. Check the Yammer Resources
   https://www.microsoft.com/en-au/microsoft-365/yammer/yammer-overview
3. Download the Yammer Adoption Playbook
   https://onedrive.live.com/view.aspx?resid=8D13E85F1CF91770!261&ithint=file%2cpptx&authkey=!AJWVvlGbbsz2ML8
4. Join the Microsoft Tech Community about Yammer
   https://techcommunity.microsoft.com/t5/yammer/ct-p/Yammer?country=AU&culture=en-au

PLANNER & TO DO

What you need to know

- Use Planner and To Do to keep track of tasks and actions
- If you love to write a task list on paper, and then draw boxes beside each item that you can tick off – To Do is for you
- If you want to visualise tasks across a process, or journey (like a Kanban board) then Planner is a good choice
- The Tasks app in Microsoft Teams consolidates any actions assigned to you in either To Do, or Planner, so you can always have an up-to-date view of what is on your plate.

Learn more about this ingredient

Microsoft To Do is a task management app that allows you to manage your tasks across devices and stay organised through your day. Create tasks, organise them into lists, add details and reminders to them as well as notes and attachments. You can also share your lists to others if they need to access and collaborate on your tasks.

To make things a little bit more exciting you are able to personalise and customise each list with backgrounds and colours that makes the entire experience of using To Do visually appealing as well as auditory with the sound of a bell when you mark off items complete.

Ding! Task completed! Is there a better sound to feel accomplished?

The value of To Do is that it is integrated with other Microsoft applications such as Outlook, Planner, and of course, Teams. For example, every time you flag an Outlook email for action, you will see it in the Flagged Email list in To Do.

Similarly, any tasks assigned to you from within Microsoft Planner are automatically seen in your To Do under the Assigned to You list.

The beauty of To Do is that it allows you to organise tasks into lists and importance. You can star mark important items or drag and drop tasks into the My Day list to create a daily action list for you to keep yourself accountable for achieving what you want in the day.

Personally, I use To Do as my personal productivity app. Everyone uses it differently so it's up to you to dabble with the recipe to find one that suits you best. Look at your life, your preferred utensils, and what you prefer to use by way of ingredients.

What do I mean by that?

Well, consider your preferred way of working and what tools you use the most (desktop, laptop, tablet, surface, or audio assistance such as Cortana) then customise to suit.

For example, the bulk of my time is spent working on desktop, so I have pinned the To Do app to my Windows desktop task bar. It is also downloaded as an app on my mobile phone.

Every morning, as I start my workday To Do is the first thing I open. I determine the critical tasks that need to be completed that day. (The critical tasks are 'starred' and listed in the *Important* bucket). Then I move those tasks to *My Day* which keeps me accountable to do these. If I do not complete the task, I move it out of *My Day* or change the due by date. I also check the tasks that have been *Assigned to Me*, what has been *Planned* and any *Emails Flagged* to determine what also gets moved to My Day.

You can even create To Do tasks directly from Microsoft Teams posts. It means that when you come across a post in a Teams channel, you can instantly create a To Do task from it.

There's no right or wrong way in using any function of Microsoft, and To Do is no different. Ultimately, it's about knowing your preferred working style, the devices you prefer to use and the habits regarding productivity and task management that is important to you. If you're not using a task management application or function in Outlook, Planner, or any third-party application, then we would recommend you check out To Do and have a dabble in it to see how you can make it work for you and your life.

Get Cooking with To Do:

1. Read more about Microsoft To Do
   https://todo.microsoft.com/tasks/
2. Download the app to your desktop and devices
3. Brainstorm some tasks you need to do this week and experiment with the various functions such as providing details, adding reminders, adding them to My Day or marking them Important with a star
4. Allocate your tasks into lists and change the background of the lists to something that is to your taste
5. Read how others are using Microsoft To Do for some ideas on how you can create your own recipes for productivity:

a. Six Tips to Make the Most of Microsoft To Do on Windows
   https://techcommunity.microsoft.com/t5/microsoft-to-do-blog/six-tips-to-make-the-most-of-microsoft-to-do-on-windows/ba-p/1578451
b. Resources on To Do: Help and Learning
   https://support.microsoft.com/en-us/todo

Where To Do is designed mainly for the individual, Planner enables us to "organise teamwork with initiative, collaborative, visual, task management."

Planner allows you to track and manage your team projects in a visual way using boards to keep your team organised. Before you ask, "Hey, isn't that like Trello?" It is, but with some slight differences. For one, it's a Microsoft product and this means it talks to other Microsoft products and is available as part of your Office 365 subscription.

Planner is a great tool to use if you don't need a heavy project management software program but need enough to be able to manage resources, people, tasks, and actions within a team.

Within each board there are cards which you can attach additional information such as:

- Details of the task
- Start & Due Dates

- Priority
- Labels
- Checklists
- Notes
- Attachments
- Comments
- Assign Members

Planner also includes a hub area where you can track the overall progress of the plan and drill down to Member, Tasks, and Calendar and create various charts that show status, buckets, and priorities. The Schedule function in Planner allows you to see the calendar of all tasks and when they're due as well as filter tasks to what is due, late, needed today, tomorrow, this and next week or unassigned.

For me, I like to use Planner as my personal learning board which I call my 'Learning Playlists'. In a way, it becomes my own professional learning board that I can add tasks to complete. (Of course, you will need to make time for learning these every day).

Many organisations are exploring ways to support their people to build a professional skill and new capabilities and to encourage self-directed learning. Managers and team leaders can enable their people to consider using Planner to create individualised personal learning boards (or team-based learning boards for that matter).

For example, the columns or 'buckets' in my own plan include the following:

- Mandatory Training to Complete
- Microsoft Product Knowledge to Learn
- Recordings to Watch or Listen to
- Books & Blogs to Read
- Presentations to Create
- Courses to Undertake
- Experiments to Try
- People to Connect With

Personally, I have found a recipe for Planner that suits me and my development needs. Given that you can also create flows and automations that feed into Planner, I have also included these into my plan. One example is that every time I see a tweet that is shared that has something I'd like to experiment or try out, I have developed a flow using PowerAutomate that recognises the hashtag #helenexperiments so that it goes directly to the board, "Tweets to Follow Up On". That way, I don't have to waste time searching for tweets as they automatically flow into the relevant board for future action.

Using Planner means that you can determine how – and if – this product is suitable for your work and team's needs. With a little creativity, you'll be able to find what suits best and how it can be used. If you're using a third-party application that does something similar, it may be time to revisit this and determine if indeed Planner can do the same functions but it's part of the Microsoft environment which means that it's linked to all your other work, too.

If you're thinking that this is something that you'd like in life outside of work, at the time of printing this book, it's not available now for consumer O365 accounts as it is reserved for business, premium and educational subscribers to Microsoft 365.

Get Cooking with Planner:

1. Get started with Microsoft Planner https://support.microsoft.com/en-us/office/sign-in-to-microsoft-planner-fe43c972-5a95-4071-86d4-423a64a3b21e

2. Join the Planner community to ask questions about how you can use it and discover new ideas and insights https://techcommunity.microsoft.com/t5/planner/bd-p/Planner

3. Check out the resources on Planner: Help and Learning https://support.microsoft.com/en-us/planner

4. Integrate your Planner plans as tabs in relevant Microsoft Teams channels

5. Find out which app is right for your project: when do you use Microsoft To Do, Planner and Project? https://support.microsoft.com/en-us/office/when-to-use-microsoft-project-planner-or-to-do-8f950d32-d5f4-40db-a8b7-4d1b82b55e17

6. Read how one of our team members are using Microsoft Planner for some ideas on how you can create your own recipes for productivity: How Helen Blunden Uses Planner to Create Personal Learning Playlists: https://activatelearning.com.au/2019/11/create-your-learning-playlist/

MICROSOFT FORMS

What you need to know

- Create forms that allow you to capture information, internally, as well as externally
- Create Quizzes for learning material, fun events or get to know you opportunities
- Share forms internally or externally and see information update live
- Connect forms to Teams Tabs for collaboration opportunities

Learn more about this ingredient

If I only had a dollar for every time I was asked to submit a survey. Although we can jest here, love them or hate them, surveys, polls and quizzes allow us to capture sentiment, results, and recommendations so that we can improve our work and processes.

Microsoft Forms is a nifty program that allows you to create a survey and questionnaire within minutes. You can then share the form to people within your organisation, or anyone with the link as a URL, embed into a webpage or a QR code. You can customise the forms to be visually appealing using the templates within or select your own background images. You can also set up the form so that you can also shuffle questions; have responses returned depending on how people answer the questions; collect and view responses in real-time visually or through Excel. You can also collaborate on the forms with your colleagues.

Different industries and teams will find their own use cases for Forms. Marketing may use them to gauge employee sentiment. IT may use them to capture some basic technical questions for their tech support requests, meanwhile small teams may even use them to determine details need for this year's Christmas party.

However, it's the educators who in our experience use Microsoft Forms in the most effective way – to assist in the assessment of their students. They share classroom quizzes to any device and use the branching within Forms to create custom tests and formative assessments that are self-graded. Some have also used Microsoft Forms to create a branched online course. The branching allows the quiz to change according to your responses to specific questions.

Using Microsoft Forms as your survey tool also enables you to receive and analyse the responses that are submitted. You can collect these responses in the form of an Excel spreadsheet or view the data in a simple dashboard format in the Responses tab.

The use of Microsoft Forms is only limited by your imagination. Everything from quizzes, sign up pages, booking sheets, polls, questionnaires, surveys or build your own branched online course.

A response to a form can even be used as a trigger to start a PowerAutomate flow – so if you are considering how you plan to automate the processing of data that you capture, Forms and PowerAutomate is a great combination.

An example would be if you created an internal customer feedback form. If a response scored lower than 6 out of 10, you could automate a notification to your department lead to proactively reach out to that individual to understand how better we could have served them

The easiest way to get started with Microsoft Forms is to add a form to a Team you are a member of. Simply add a Tab to the channel. You (and the other members of your Team) will then be able to collaborate on building your form, and you all have access to the data collected. We use this approach regularly to capture information during projects. Everyone on the project (who is a member of the Team) can see the data, and in real time. Not just the person who has the survey link.

Time to get cooking and consider how you can use this tool in your own work and projects.

Get Cooking with Microsoft Forms:

1. Read the Ultimate Guide in Using Microsoft Forms
   https://collab365.community/ultimate-guide-
   microsoft-forms/
2. Read how to integrate Forms into other Microsoft
   products https://support.microsoft.com/en-
   us/office/integration-fd5521ec-bd27-48ee-8aad-
   84ffe95c2a8b?ocid=oo_support_mix_marvel_ups_s
   upport_socformspromo&ui=en-US&rs=en-
   US&ad=US

POWER APPS

What you need to know

- PowerApps allows you to create custom mobile or web-based experiences
- If you are confident in working with complex formulars in Excel, you may find the path towards developing simple solutions in PowerApps straight forward. For most of us, it will require some dedicated learning
- Whilst PowerApps is a powerful platform to develop and deploy applications aligned to your specific business processes, they do have some licensing implications. It is best to explore with your IT team and get their advice along the way.

Learn more about this ingredient

In our roles as consultants, one of the key remits is to coach and educate our clients on use of the Microsoft 365 gamut of technologies for better communication, collaboration, and just getting stuff done.

We are not tech heads by any stretch of the imagination. Trust us when I say that we are on the people side! But you will agree that we must give it to technology when it acts as an enabler and significantly helps our day-to-day tasks become so much more stream-lined and easier.

At the dizzying rate at which Microsoft churns out technological capabilities and improvements, it has become prudent for us keep our pulse on 'What's New in M365', and how this would create efficiencies for our clients in their world.

One such capability, or rather suite of capabilities, is the Power Platform. The Power Platform is Microsoft's low-code/no-code range of offerings that enable 'citizen developers' in any organisation to develop applications, solutions, automate many of those tedious business processes, and do cool dashboard style reporting, quickly. The plus-point is that it easily connects to as many data sources of your preference just by two simple clicks (at the time of drafting this book, it comes with ~350 out of the box connectors, so higher probability that most of your data sources could be connected, otherwise you can create your own). It can sit across the top of Office 365, Dynamic 365, Azure, and other standalone applications.

In 2019, Microsoft's CEO Satya Nadella announced that nearly 500 million new applications will be built in the next five years alone. That is, more than the number of applications built collectively in the last 40 years! If that is not an indication of what is to come, I cannot say what is. Also, Gartner predicted that 65% of enterprise application development will be in the low-code category by 2024. You can read more of this at: https://www.gartner.com/en/documents/3991199/mag ic-quadrant-for-enterprise-low-code-application-platf

What does this mean? More budget needed? Should you be picking up the phone and dialling HR right away to ensure you are resourced with an army of skilled application developers? Does your company's budget need to be augmented to cater for these new recruits?

Luckily, no. More likely than not, *you already have the skills*. If you have used the drag and drop capabilities in Microsoft PowerPoint, inserted media, and formatted shapes, then that is a good starting point. Also, if you have used formulas in Excel, then you have a solid base to start off with. All you need is an attitude to give it a go! The sugar on top is that they come in ready with hundreds of pre-built templates. It is your choice to start from nothing or start from a template and customise it as you need.

Under the Microsoft Power Platform umbrella, there are three main components called Power Apps, PowerAutomate, and Power BI. We will elaborate on PowerApps in this chapter, and PowerAutomate and PowerBI in the following chapters.

PowerApps allows you, or anyone in your organisation with the appropriate permissions, to create simple, yet powerful applications that others can interact with, that can be accessed on a browser, tablet, or a mobile device. You do not need to be an accomplished developer or have prior experience in coding.

Let us talk about why we need Power Apps in the first place, and is it worth investing your time?

We know by now that they allow us to create beautiful mobile applications, sometimes in a matter of minutes.

It not only helps business users but also people like you and me who may not know how to create apps.

When it comes to businesses, there are several reasons why they are taking to Microsoft Power Apps.

Firstly, a lot of customer business apps are often not ready to run across multiple devices. Particularly if your organisation runs legacy applications. Making your app run across multiple devices can be difficult, and often need skilled programmers for the maintenance and upkeep of the application. However, that is where Microsoft Power Apps shines. You can quickly create an app to serve a particular business need, without the need to break the bank on an expensive custom-built application or jump through several hoops to get your business case approved. This allows you to free up time of your skilled resources and utilise them for more value-add tasks. Win-win.

Secondly, they can connect to hundreds of data sources, again reducing expensive storage requirements if the application is meant for internal organisational use.

Thirdly, it helps streamline business processes and makes the lives of staff much easier. A common application of this we come across is for organisations that may have field workers who go out and need to report issues back to their supervisor in the office. Rather than having to wait till they get back or sending emails backwards and forwards, they can simply use a Power App to capture all the necessary information and initiate the relevant business process right from where they are.

Another topical example is to use as a Staff Health Check-in app when clocking into work, notifying management if they are feeling unwell or any symptoms of late or have been to a Covid-19 hot-spot recently.

Get Cooking with Power Apps:

1. Watch a video on how to create your Microsoft Power App.
   https://docs.microsoft.com/en-us/learn/paths/create-powerapps/

2. Watch how to Create a Canvas App
   https://docs.microsoft.com/en-us/learn/paths/create-powerapps/

3. Watch how to Use basic formulas in Power Apps
   https://docs.microsoft.com/en-us/learn/paths/use-basic-formulas-powerapps-canvas-app/

4. Watch how to Use UI and Controls in a Canvas App
   https://docs.microsoft.com/en-us/learn/paths/ui-controls-canvas-app-powerapps/

5. Undertake the Free Virtual App in a Day Workshop
   https://powerusers.microsoft.com/t5/Webinars-and-Video-Gallery/App-in-a-Day-Free-Training-Class-to-Learn-PowerApps/td-p/318794

6. Access the Microsoft Power Apps Learning Resources
   https://powerapps.microsoft.com/en-us/blog/microsoft-powerapps-learning-resources/

POWERAUTOMATE

What you need to know

- Automate repetitive tasks with PowerAutomate
- There are hundreds of templates you can start with, which means you could have common processes automated within minutes
- There are hundreds of connectors which you can use to automate inputs from or outputs to 3rd party systems (some free, some paid).

Learn more about this ingredient

Sometimes the processes within our work are repetitive and tedious. I paid attention to this when I realised I was consistently and repeatedly doing tasks that over the years became habit but were serving me no other purpose other than frustrating me. For example, spending time creating folders in Outlook and manually moving emails to them.

Similarly, it made me pay attention to how everyone else was working and what tasks were asked of me repeatedly by team members.

"Send me that email every week!"

"Save that email to the relevant channel in Microsoft Teams!"

"Respond to that person and cc me every time you send them that document!"

"Check that survey daily to see if anyone has responded!"

And so on.

I started to question why we were doing the things we were doing in the same way and getting frustrated that we had no hours in the day to do more value-added work.

In the past, when we didn't have the choice we do today to streamline our repetitive and dare I say it, mundane tasks, it makes no sense to continue these when we have tools at our fingertips to make our life easier.

Something had to give or else I was going to go nuts with wasting an inordinate amount of time on administrative and routine tasks.

So, one day, I took note of what tasks I was doing every 15 minutes and that's when I realised that at certain times of the day for certain tasks, I was wasting time trying to find information or alternatively, I seemed to be the "conduit" between devices or applications speaking with each other. I had to take the 'middleperson' (me) out of the equation to get some of my time back and focus on more value-added work.

Enter Microsoft PowerAutomate.

Microsoft PowerAutomate allows you to create automated workflows that streamline your workday.

In my role as Community Manager, I set up automatic reminders for tasks; streamlined the flow of information such as emails to automatically flow into the relevant Microsoft Teams channels; created a way to capture contact details of people I network with at conferences and events and automated some business processes such as request for technical assistance for my Community.

This saved me time to focus on less repetitive tasks and more value-added ones that require time for me to think, plan, co-ordinate, and manage.

By letting go of the small administrative tasks "to the machine", I felt that I could focus on the main aspect of my role which was to manage and build the community. After all, that was what I was employed to do, not waste my day with administrative tasks that served no purpose other than to frustrate me.

So, what are flows in Microsoft PowerAutomate?

Flows are triggered by certain events that you configure in PowerAutomate that set off a series of actions under certain conditions.

For example, you can have a flow that sends you daily reminders of the weather in your city; or that pings you whenever someone has responded to an important survey you sent out. You can even automate emails that you send out on a regular basis.

Out of sight, out of mind!

Flows can be automated, triggered instantly, or scheduled at certain times.

Similarly, there are others known as button flows that can be set off with a tap of a button on your mobile device.

You can also use Microsoft PowerAutomate to create business process flows to ensure that the same process is followed by everyone in your company or UI Flows that record the clicks and keyboard strokes from your desktop and web applications and then automate the playback of manual steps on your legacy software, There's a whole lot more to write about Microsoft PowerAutomate because the tool is so in-depth however the intention of this book is to get you "dabbling in the kitchen" instead of becoming "Head Chef". That would come with time, experience, training, and motivation to take your Microsoft PowerAutomate skills to the next level. For now, focus on what you can automate simply using some of the templates that Microsoft provide that will make your own work life easier.

So, Microsoft PowerAutomate allows you to create workflows without the need of any coding experience. You can build your own or you can use the myriad of template that are already within the system that you can use as is or configure to your specific needs. Start dabbling and see what you can automate today.

Get Cooking with PowerAutomate:

1. Get started by checking out the Microsoft PowerAutomate Documentation where you can work through the links on this page to get you started
   https://docs.microsoft.com/en-us/power-automate/?utm_source=flow-sidebar&utm_medium=web
2. Undertake the Introduction to PowerAutomate course in Microsoft Learn
   https://docs.microsoft.com/en-us/learn/browse/?products=power-automate

POWER BI

Learn more about this ingredient

When people provide reasons for using Power BI, it's often at the expense of Excel. You and I both know almost every organisation in the world relies on Excel to build business critical models and reports. Don't get me wrong, I am a big Excel fan. For years, Excel was the only app on my desktop that could crunch numbers and make charts.

So up until Power BI was released, if someone needed a report, I did what everyone else did. I took the raw data, I did some data cleansing and formatting, threw in a few VLOOKUPs for good measure, added a pivot table or two, and (almost) just like that – report ready!

Did these reports provide well organised, accurate information that enabled decisions to be made? You bet they did. What's the problem then?

Good news first. Excel is not the problem; Excel still works great. The better news is that you now have a new tool, Power BI, which allows you to present a certain type of report in a way that changes the game. Let's look at an example.

You are producing a monthly sales report across your organisation. The data comes from multiple, frequently updated data sources. The audience is segmented across the organisation and includes the executive and various levels of management. We want one report where the executive sees all data across all locations, area managers just their areas, and managers just their stores. This is already looking like time-consuming task for Excel. Now, take this up several more notches and start thinking about reports that are self-served by the audience with the expectation of (near) real-time reporting, now add the ability to drill down into data, or leverage machine learning to summarise the content being presented.

So, Microsoft Power BI is the tool of choice when you want to:

- Create and distribute reports that are web based
- Provide reports that are permissioned so that a person's level of access governs the content they can access
- Generate reports that look good on any smart device
- Enable users to explore and interrogate data to access required insights on the fly

- Support real time data refresh
- Reporting that requires an element of 'guidance' or 'story telling'. Power BI can guide and drive the user experience
- Create a quick report from a cloud app like Xero, Salesforce or SAP
- Provide one or more 'master datasets' that will allow people in your organisation to build their own reports from approved, accurate data
- Draw data from multiple datasets (and the data is stored in different platforms)

Finally, don't think of this as Power BI versus Excel – you'll get the best results by knowing which tool to use when.

If you'd like to see some sample Power BI reports online, the Microsoft Power BI Community https://community.powerbi.com/t5/Data-Stories-Gallery/bd-p/DataStoriesGallery provides some great examples.

Get Cooking with Power BI:

1. Power BI is not a single app but a business intelligence platform. It is good to understand the components before you get started.

2. If you're an Excel user, then you can get up and running quickly. Here's a foundation course that walks you through the basics.

VIVA INSIGHTS

What you need to know

- Reflect on your own practice and improve your time management or work/life boundaries – based on how you use Office 365.
- Put into practice a 'virtual commute' to help you bookend your workday, or set aside time to focus on key activities
- Understand the key relationships you have within the organisation

Learn more about this ingredient

I had a chuckle this morning as I checked my Twitter threads. A person in my network had tweeted:

"Just received my weekly "Microsoft Viva Insights" update from Microsoft Office. It is exciting that they are

focused on my wellbeing, my ability to focus and my collaboration network."

Now this may have been made in jest, maybe even facetiously, as it was hard to tell in their tweet... but let's explore what Microsoft Viva Insights (one of the four modules of Microsoft's Employee Experience Platform Microsoft Viva) is and how it is more about Microsoft providing us with some data which helps us make informed choices about how we focus on our work, who we are collaborating with, and what actions we need to take concerning our wellbeing. Viva Insights uses the 'digital exhaust' of your work – the signals that point to when you log in, when you log out, how often you check email, who you collaborate with etc, and present them in a way that allows you to understand how you work every day. For example, how much time do you have in your calendar that will enable you to focus on a specific activity? Or how much of your time is spent in meetings? Armed with these insights, you can make informed choices about how you approach your work.

Now, like anything, Microsoft is only able to show data if you are using other Microsoft products. Therefore, if you're spending time in other tools and platforms outside of the Microsoft ecosphere, consider that the data it returns may not provide a true and accurate picture, so bear this in mind.

Microsoft Viva Insights welcomes you to "Discover Your Habits and Work Smarter."

First things first, you'll need to configure your work week. For me, I work three days a week and I want to be able to get an accurate picture of where I'm spending most of my time. Change your work week and time zones in the Configuration Settings. While you're there, you can decide if you want Microsoft Analytics to automatically book focus times into your calendar. What does this mean? Well, you'll see one-hour blocks of Focus Time that magically appear in your calendar that you can choose to use – or like me, move them around to times most appropriate in your calendar. Or of course you can turn them off.

The Microsoft Viva Insights Home Page is a dashboard of the hours and percentages you spent doing the following in the last four weeks:

a) *Focus time*: How much time you have available to focus

b) *Quiet Days*: How many days you had without interruptions to disconnect and recharge.

c) *Network*: How many people you have contacted through emails, chats, and calls.

d) *Collaboration*: The percentage of time you spent time in meetings.

Drilling down into each area, Microsoft Analytics provides additional details and recommendations that you can explore and see trends. It provides suggestions for you to consider improving your statistics and think about how you can work smarter by rediscovering where time and productivity is lost.

Before you think negatively that Microsoft Viva Insights tracks your work, think about the positive benefits it provides. Too often, we are unaware of where our time disappears to during the day as we have no accurate picture of what applications we were in the most, who we collaborated with, and how often we were doing work or taking calls outside of work hours.

Microsoft Viva Insights allows you to get a view on tracking your time and progress – it is where you can see the reason of your lack of progress on goals because it's there in black and white.

The data tells the story of your week and your month. Sometimes it makes for some sobering reading. Other times, you can see areas for improvement yourself.

Personally, I love Microsoft Viva Insights and every month, I review my progress across the four areas to consider the following questions:

- Do I have enough uninterrupted time to get my work done?
- Am I able to disconnect and recharge?
- Do I proactively manage my network?
- Could my time working with others be more productive?

Consider encouraging your team members to check their Microsoft Viva Insights when they can as it forces them to reflect on their work and see areas of improvement.

Get Cooking with Microsoft Viva Insights:

1. Check out Microsoft Viva Insights in www.office.com or use Improve Employee Wellbeing | Microsoft Viva Insights and now spend some time scrutinising your work patterns for the last four weeks on the dashboard. I mean, really scrutinising it
   a. What are the patterns you're seeing?
   b. Are you surprised with the data it's showing you?
   c. How can you use the suggestions it's providing you to change your work patterns and behaviours for the next four weeks?
   d. Go have a cup of coffee or a meditation moment if you've seen hairy and scary numbers that are telling you that your focus and wellbeing is out of control
2. Get the Microsoft Viva Insights into your MS Outlook https://docs.microsoft.com/en-AU/viva/insights/personal/Briefing/be-overview?culture=en-au&country=AU
3. Frequently asked questions about Microsoft Viva Insights https://docs.microsoft.com/en-

au/viva/insights/use/my-team-faqanalytics/myanalytics/overview/mya-faq

4. Read how leaders and managers can use the productivity, wellbeing, and focus insights in Microsoft Teams

5. https://docs.microsoft.com/en-AU/viva/insights/Use/viva-insights-intro

6. Navigate the Microsoft Viva Insights dashboard

7. https://docs.microsoft.com/en-au/viva/insights/personal/use/dashboard-2

VIVA LEARNING

What you need to know

- Access free learning content from content providers like LinkedIn Learning the context of your work
- Curate learning paths from across subscriptions that your organisation has access to.

Learn more about this ingredient

Microsoft Viva Learning is a centralised learning hub that sits in Microsoft Teams where you can access free (and enterprise or premium resources) learning experience when you need them. Microsoft Viva Learning is one of the four modules of Microsoft Viva, the new employee experience platform for Microsoft.

Viva Learning allows you to incorporate learning into your work every day. If you don't know how to do a certain skill or if you need to qualify for your Microsoft certification, you are able to do this and more through Viva Learning. Some of the functions you will find are:

- Search specific learning content relevant to your needs, role, and career
- Share and recommend learning content to other team members, channels, and teams
- Browse courses from LinkedIn Learning, Microsoft 365 Training, Coursera, EdX and Skillsoft as well as other third-party providers your organisation may have subscriptions with.
-

As mentioned in our chapter on Continuous Learning and Development, knowledge workers nowadays will need to take charge of their own personal and professional development to keep up with the constant change in their workplace. Through Viva Learning, you will be able to do this – all without leaving Microsoft Teams.

Get Cooking with Microsoft Viva Learning:

1. Read about Microsoft Viva Learning https://docs.microsoft.com/en-au/microsoft-

365/learning/overview-viva-learning?view=o365-worldwide and
https://www.microsoft.com/en-au/microsoft-viva/learning?rtc=1

2. View the Microsoft Viva Learning Overview
https://www.microsoft.com/en-au/microsoft-viva/learning?rtc=1

3. Watch the Microsoft Viva Learning Deep Dive
https://www.microsoft.com/en-au/microsoft-viva/learning?rtc=1

VIVA TOPICS

What you need to know

- Acronyms, buzz words, or corporate lingo are difficult to get your head around
- Use Viva topics to automatically discover, and then curate resources around these specific topics
- Connect people in your organisation to the resources and subject matter experts, simply by moving your mouse over a key word

Learn more about this ingredient

In the course of your everyday work, you may have come across a term in your documents and files that you were unaware of and wanted to know more about and who was involved. It could have been the name of a project or a subject or term that your organisation shares and uses. You may have spent an inordinate amount of time searching for this term across your intranet and other documentation to learn more. A recent addition to Microsoft's Modern Work story, Viva Topics can help you organise knowledge and experts across your organisation. Your knowledge managers or other experts can then refine these topics through topic pages while artificial intelligence learns from their input. What this means is that your organisation can build an effective knowledge base which is easily discoverable through the apps you use by the topic cards and Microsoft Search.

For organisations that are focused on leveraging their organisational knowledge, or better managing the intellectual property they have, Viva Topics is a terrific way to systematically surface knowledge in the context of work.

In part two of this book, we will talk about the importance of content discovery and curation and a modern workplace skill. Even though at the time of publishing this book, Microsoft Viva Topics was still new, and we were learning about its applications however, it shouldn't stop you from discovering more about what it is and how it can help your organisation.

Get Cooking with Microsoft Viva Topics:

1. Read about Microsoft Viva Topics and see it in action https://www.microsoft.com/en-au/microsoft-viva/topics

2. Read and watch the Microsoft Viva Topics Overview https://docs.microsoft.com/en-AU/microsoft-365/knowledge/topic-experiences-overview

3. Read how Microsoft Viva Topics enables discovery and curation https://docs.microsoft.com/en-au/microsoft-365/knowledge/topic-experiences-discovery-curation

4. Get started with Microsoft Viva Topics adoption https://docs.microsoft.com/en-au/microsoft-365/knowledge/topics-adoption-getstarted

VIVA CONNECTIONS

What you need to know

- Employees are always wanting to know more and be informed of what is happening around them
- Viva Connections allows communicators to surface important content via your intranet, on your mobile via the Microsoft Teams app
- There is a dashboard, as well as a feed that blends both structured, and unstructured information

Learn more about this ingredient

Microsoft Viva Connections allows you to keep informed with what is happening across your organisation through an individually tailored feed that includes organisational as well as employee contributions.

Think of it as a place to get your news of the day or to catch up with what's happening in your organisation. In other words, your intranet that you can access directly within Microsoft Teams. At the time of writing, Microsoft Viva Connections is still a relatively new product and as such we will be exploring its capabilities in coming months. We see some enormous potential though for organisations that want to create personalised experiences for their employees. This could blend:

- High level data from your HR system that highlights current leave balances

- Lightweight processes that employees need to engage with for compliance reasons – for example COVID office check ins

- Executive leadership communications from SharePoint or Yammer

- Learning content.

Get Cooking with Microsoft Viva Connections:

1. Read an overview of Viva Connections
   https://docs.microsoft.com/en-us/viva/connections/viva-connections-overview

2. Watch how employees use Microsoft Viva Connections
   https://www.youtube.com/watch?v=f_PkVcn6gxk

3. Watch how leaders could use Microsoft Viva Connections
   https://www.youtube.com/watch?v=jFfzB2t9qkc

Now that we have explored the different ingredients you have at your fingertips, lets now turn our attention to the skills that you need to make those ingredients shine.

PART TWO:
SKILLS

Recipes have played an important part in our daily lives. Whether they involve food, family, or work. Just look at the myriad of articles, video, podcasts, books, and recordings that tell us the magical ingredients that go towards creating the perfect meal, or life. Although these recipes assist us in some ways, they also miss the mark at other times. Let me explain.

I grew up in a Greek household where food and family were central to how we communicated and socialised. Food was what brought people together to share stories and laughter. (At times, it was also what broke them apart especially between proud mothers who were determined that their spanakopita was better than anyone else's spanakopita).

Quibbles aside, when the tables were laden with delicious Greek delicacies, my cousins and I knew exactly which mother cooked what dish because each had her own specialty and manner of preparing the meal that was unique and distinctive from each other. (Hence the rivalry).

For some, it was how the dish was prepared, for others it was the quality and quantity of local organic produce, herbs and spices, while for others it was using the traditional methods which varied from region to region and in many cases, from village to village.

To keep the recipe in the family so that I could create the same meals when my mother was no longer with me, I asked for her recipes and one day, we wrote these down in a notebook. Imagine my frustration when she would not provide me with exact measurements.

"It is about a beer cup of flour," she would say.

"What on earth is a beer cup?" I'd ask.

She would fling open one of the kitchen cupboards and show me an old cup she used to drink beer from back in 1985 and put it into my hand.

"I don't drink beer from this cup!" I exclaimed.

"Well, it's what I use for this recipe. Fill this cup with flour then I might sprinkle a bit more."

This would frustrate me as I wanted *exact* measurements.

"Mum, I'll have to measure this out with some flour now and weigh it," while I searched for measuring cups and weighing scales. She would roll her eyes at me and add, "Sometimes you just need to go by feel and by making the meal. The more you do this recipe, you will learn what is the right amount for you."

This statement got me thinking.

In a time where in our work and our life, we want certainty, we rely on others to provide us with the recipes that will enable us to have that perfect experience. However, they always seem to miss the mark somewhat. We rely on others to provide us with the hard facts, data, and statistics to support the reason for doing something so we can replicate success. However, we miss out on something in the process, and that is the experience of experimenting, trying things out for ourselves, and making our own interpretation of the recipe that is distinctive to us.

In this chapter, we will explore some of the skills and capabilities you can build to enable that experimentation to happen. So that you can use Microsoft 365 in ways that benefit you and your organisation and create distinctive experiences. Not only for your teams, but also for you individually.

We have given you the recipes in these books to help you move from simply looking at tools like Microsoft Teams as a place for teamwork and collaboration to instead, a pathway of possibility beyond your team and organisation. Taking a longer and more strategic view from team to one of creating impact in your organisation, community, and even society.

To do this, you will need new skills and capabilities. Like a commis chef who has completed their basic training in a kitchen, so have you on Microsoft Teams.

It is now time to sharpen that knife and make these recipes your own.

Let's get started.

How to Use This Part

We will explore a variety to topics in this part that relate to building new skills and capabilities that will help you in your work.

However, it is not what you think. It is not about learning new technical and developer skills so that you can become a jet developer of Microsoft applications and bots (although this may be the outcome if you want this), it is more about giving you the skills that will serve you to achieve an outcome. You may wish to call them the "soft skills". Regardless, these skills can be applied in any context and manner, and as such we will also give you some activities that you can do individually and with your team to explore these further.

Our aim is to have you use the recipes in our book but in the process, break them down, recreate them, change them, make them your own, and then like my mother, share them with others so that others can do the same.

For every activity, we encourage you to reflect on the process and share your learning to others whether it is in your Teams channels, across your organisation in your Yammer communities, or the world in your social networks and online communities.

Through sharing comes conversations of shared experiences and possibilities of collaboration and co-operation of projects that will support change on a wider scale.

> *"The future belongs to those who learn more skills and combine them in creative ways."*
> – Robert Greene

FOCUS, TIME MANAGEMENT & BOUNDARIES

Learn more about this skill

"The bad news is time flies. The good news is you're the pilot."
– Michael Altshuler

You might think it is strange to start off with this topic, however, you only have to look at the immense changes our world has seen with the pandemic to realise that workers have had to negotiate not only a move to remote work but also navigate a balance between the demands of home schooling their children or looking after loved ones.

We heard stories in the media that people felt "zoomed out" as they replaced their face-to-face meetings with back-to-back online and virtual meetings and subsequently suffering from meeting fatigue.

Research from the Human Factors Lab in the article, "The Future of Work – the Good, the Challenging and the Unknown" (https://www.microsoft.com/en-us/microsoft-365/blog/2020/07/08/future-work-good-challenging-unknown/) showed that overwork and stress was higher in video meetings than non-meeting work such as writing emails. Stress began to set in about two hours into the day because people had to focus continuously on the screen to stay engaged and read cues.

Making boundaries to manage your time, attention and focus is one of the key aspects you will need to master so that you're freed up mentally to focus on building new skills. Your boundaries could be physical (whether or not you work in an open plan space, or have an office with a door), temporal (the time of day you start and stop work), or psychological (thinking or not thinking about work). How often work (or life) passes through these boundaries will have an impact on whether you achieve your professional or personal goals.

To assist you in navigating your boundaries with work, you can use Viva Insights. As described in a previous chapter, Viva Insights is a personal productivity analytics tool that explores your work patterns and can provide insight on how to improve your focus, wellbeing, network, and collaboration. These insights are presented via a dashboard accessible via your browser, a weekly email, and via the Viva

Insights app in Microsoft Teams. To learn more, refer back to the Viva Insights chapter in the Part One.

Get Cooking with Viva Insights:

1. Go to https://insights.viva.office.com, click on "Personal" and explore your work patterns for the last four weeks. Consider how much time you are spending in each of the four segments of Focus, Wellbeing, Network and Collaboration and ask yourself:
   a. Do you have enough uninterrupted time to get your work done?
   b. Are you able to disconnect and recharge?
   c. Do you proactively manage your network?
   d. Could your time working with others be more productive?

If your answers are surprising to you, then it may be time to look at making some boundaries to manage your time, attention, and focus.

If you do not have Microsoft Viva Insights available, then don't stress. You can use other means to be able to capture what you are doing at any one time in your day. For example, capture what you are doing every 15 minutes in a notebook, an app or even an Excel spreadsheet and categorise into those four buckets. At the end of the week, you'll be able to see where your time is being spent. Alternatively, explore some apps that will be able to track time and generate a report for you.

After you have explored your report, it's time for some action. Here is what you can do as a start:

1. Explore the recommendations in your Viva Insights Report and explore the various suggestions it makes related to Focus, Wellbeing, Network, and Collaboration
2. Set up your Focus Plan in Viva Insights by customising the plan to your needs. Under *Microsoft Viva Insights > Focus> Plan Configuration*, change the days as well as automatically have Microsoft Viva Insights block out Focus Time in your calendar. If you don't want it to set focus time automatically, you can choose to have reminders to do this
3. Undertake a "Notifications Audit" across all your Microsoft tools and determine which notifications are critical and which can be turned off for your desktop and mobile applications
4. Create space by using the Status field in Microsoft Teams to change your availability to Do Not Disturb, Busy, Be Right Back or Available and write a message to others to explain
5. Use PowerAutomate to create buttons on your mobile phone to:

a. Block out your calendar for the next hour instantly

    i. https://flow.microsoft.com/en-us/galleries/public/templates/0a90717 32e5c445dafe8cf5113b3fa94/block-out-my-outlookcom-calendar-for-an-hour/

b. Set yourself a reminder for 10 minutes (you can change the time to whatever time you want to focus) https://australia.flow.microsoft.com/en-us/galleries/public/templates/2ec8fd1095d71 1e69e6b05429ec0d0d7/send-myself-a-reminder-in-10-minutes/

c. Report current location and activity https://australia.flow.microsoft.com/en-us/galleries/public/templates/14e9803471094 c1297cec9e6b0cb6a6d/report-current-location-and-activity/

d. Automate your out-of-office message if you've forgotten to turn it on in Microsoft Outlook by creating a flow in Microsoft PowerAutomate.

BUILDING YOUR NETWORKS

Learn more about this skill

"The currency of real networking is not greed but generosity."
– Keith Ferrazzi

Think back to a time in your life when you had a problem to overcome, a complex project to plan and co-ordinate, or a niggling issue that refused to budge from your mind.

It is likely that to determine what you needed to do, you would have referred to Google or YouTube for an approach to take or spoken to a colleague, friend, or spouse about it. However, what if it required some deeper understanding of the topic and where you didn't have the knowledge, skills, experiences, resources, or people who could help you with it?

In my previous working life as a Learning and Development consultant in corporate organisations, I had these situations happen to me often enough to sit up and realise that there was something missing from my own skillset that was holding me back from progressing in my career. Certain work situations made me realise I had to face up to and overcome some fears.

For example, an increasing amount of technology change in my field was making my subject matter expertise in adult learning practices redundant. Added to this, I had little knowledge or experience of social and virtual technologies that were taking the business and education fields by storm. I had to face the fact that what I learned at school and university many years ago was not going to serve me anymore.

There was a disconnect – a gap – that was growing every day, and which highlighted that my self-anointed claim of being an 'expert' in learning and development was indeed wrong. I was no expert. I was a fraud! How can I claim to be an expert when I had little to no knowledge or experience of the latest trends and practices in my field?

It dawned on me that I had to start from nothing again and be a learner again. And to be continually learning now for the rest of my life.

This presented a scary challenge to me because my question was, "Where do I start?" If the world is in constant change, how do I know what to focus my time and attention on?

I sat down and brainstormed a list of topics that I wanted to learn about in my professional role as a

Learning and Development consultant. I remember the list well because it included the following:

1. Artificial Intelligence for Identifying Performance Gaps in the Workplace
2. Gamification in Learning
3. Chat Bots for Delivery of Learning Resources
4. Community Management & Building
5. Yammer for Building Communities of Practice
6. Virtual Conferencing for Hybrid Learning Delivery
7. Augmented Reality
8. Virtual Reality
9. Social Learning
10. Educational Technology: Apps that Support Novel Ways to Build Peer Learning
11. MOOCs (Massive Open and Online Courses)
12. Connectivism – New skill for Modern Workers
13. Twitter – Use of Social Media and Networks for Professional Development
14. Maker Spaces
15. 'Third Places'
16. Induction & Onboarding Using Virtual Technology

I looked at my massive list and started to panic. There was too much there to learn – there simply was not enough time in my day to learn it all.

At the time, I stumbled upon the work of Harold Jarche, whose blog Life in Perpetual Beta changed my mindset. You can read his blog at https://jarche.com/.

I felt I was in a constant liminal state – perpetual beta – where I was fighting to hold onto the knowledge I gained from my experience in learning and development but at the same time wanting to let go of it and explore possibilities. Reading Harold's work showed me the importance of building a personal learning network – a network of people who you know, like, and trust, who could help you learn.

Rather than delving into each of the topics and trying to become an expert in each of them, I had to instead, look to my own network and see who fitted those criteria.

Rather than get lost in the abundant resources that are online, all I had to do was follow people who were trusted authorities in their fields or who had an interest and motivation in the topic areas I wanted to learn about, who actively showed and shared their work and thinking in this area. They would be far more useful to me to build my own knowledge as they would be the ones to point me to the best resources, the best papers, the best websites, and other trusted sources. They would save me time because they would be my information filter.

That's when the penny dropped.

I looked at my own network and realised I didn't know anyone who even had any of these skills or knowledge areas for the topics I wanted to explore. Another limitation was that I was that I surrounded myself with people who had similar skills, experiences, and mindsets to me.

The solution was obvious. I had to build a new network.

This started me on the journey of learning more about the theory of 'connectivism', a theoretical framework for understanding learning in the digital age that emphasises how digital technologies and social networks contribute to new ways of learning.

The term was first introduced by Stephen Downes and George Siemens who explained it as "the starting point of learning is the individual who feeds information into the network, which feeds information back to individuals who in turn feeds information back into the network as part of a cycle."

I thought that if I were to become a better in my work, I had to become a better learner.

To become a better learner, I had to become a better networker.

To become a better networker, I had to give to the network and not just take from it.

It was all beginning to make sense to me.

I set out to build a personal network that included people from the diverse topics I wrote about. I shared their posts on social networks; I read and commented on their blogs; I offered to help them when they asked for it. Over time, they built trust in me, and my own work and I knew that I had people to go to if I had a question specifically related to their subject or domain expertise.

The process of building a network made me realise that learning doesn't just happen individually – it can also happen with a group of people – both within and most importantly, external to my organisation and who are weak ties to me, supported and assisted by technology to store, access, and retrieve knowledge when and how I need it.

At the time of writing, Microsoft had launched Microsoft Viva, an employee experience platform which empowers people and teams with knowledge, learning and expertise in the flow of their everyday work. It uses "advanced artificial intelligence from the Microsoft Graph" (or in other words, understands how people work using Office 365) to help identify experts on specific topics in your organisation and surface knowledge through interactive experiences. It can be used to create automatic topic pages and knowledge centres that curates people, topics, and content.

But will Microsoft Viva put an end to the need of building personal networks when the "machine" does it for us?

No, we don't think so at all. In fact, our human skills will be needed more than ever.

Harold Jarche in Building Trust and Embrace Networks in Managing Complexity https://jarche.com/2014/07/build-trust-embrace-networks-manage-complexity/ explains it this way. "The new work structures required for increasingly complex networked economies need to be supported by skilled workers with the right tools. We know that sharing complex knowledge requires strong interpersonal relationships, with shared values, concepts, and mutual trust. But discovering innovative ideas usually comes via loose personal ties and diverse networks. Knowledge intensive organizations need to be structured for both. Effective knowledge-sharing drives business value in a complex economy and this requires a workforce that is adept at sense-making."

If anything, it will highlight the need for us to look at skills we need to build for our new hybrid workplaces, understand who we relate to and to place more value on the weaker, looser ties in our networks so they're more likely to bring us new insights and perspectives to serve us for the future.

That means, as humans we still need to put in the work to build that trust and generosity to collaborate and co-operate to solve for complex problems we face in our work and life – and that's why we wrote this book!

Get Cooking:

1. If you haven't filled out your Office profile, now would be the time to do it. Go to Update your

profile (microsoft.com) to find out how. Fill in your contact details and include details about your projects, your skills and expertise, interests and hobbies, and school and education as much as possible. While you're at it, write about the areas and topics that you'd like to learn more about. Your profile is searchable and discoverable. It provides others a snapshot of your expertise and areas you'd like to build upon

2. While you're at it, do the same in LinkedIn and build yourself, or refine your existing LinkedIn profile. Here's a great place to start to do this: https://www.linkedin.com/learning/learning-linkedin-3/get-started-with-linkedin

3. If you have an enterprise social network such as Yammer, explore the communities that are in it and join the ones that are interesting for you. Try every day to like a post, reply to a post, share an article of interest, or follow someone. Focus on "being interested", not "being interesting". This is a fantastic way to build trust and reputation. Also explore the Yammer Groups which are external Yammer communities that sit outside your company network. Contributing to Yammer discussions is a terrific way to build your network and tap into expertise across different jobs, industries, interest groups and countries

4. With your team, why not create a visual map of your Personal Learning Network? You can use Microsoft Whiteboard, OneNote or any mind mapping tool to map it and then share this with your team for discussion. Do others have the knowledge, skills and experience that can fill in the gaps of your map? Here's an article I wrote about how you can do this: https://activatelearning.com.au/2015/07/how-to-map-your-personal-learning-network-using-mind-maps-and-twitter-lists/

5. Start using social networks such as Twitter, not to share what you had for lunch but to start building a personal or professional network. If you find social networks overwhelming, consider using some templates in PowerAutomate to feed relevant articles with specific keywords or posts from your personal network to stem the flow

6. Insert the RSS feed of the best articles or posts that come from your personal networks into a relevant channel in Microsoft Teams, on boards in Microsoft Planner or in folders in Outlook so that it is collected and curated in one area that you can visit rather than looking for these across the web. Check out what Power Platform connectors there are that you can use to automate this process

7. Want to know more about Microsoft Viva? Check out the resources here

    https://www.microsoft.com/en-us/microsoft-viva

SHOWING & SHARING YOUR WORK

Learn more about this skill

"Make stuff you love and talk about stuff you love, and you'll attract people who love that kind of stuff. It is that simple."
– Austin Kleon

Before you say, "a good chef never reveals their secrets," I would like to reveal that sometimes the best dining experiences have been when you and friends created a meal together in the kitchen. Think about a time when you have done this. Chances are you learned something about your friends, you heard a story about how they chose the recipe, and you watched them prepare the ingredients and the meal. It is likely they learned something from you when you showed them why you cut the vegetables in one way and not the other.

Showing and sharing the process of your work and thinking openly and transparently is a recipe for effective teamwork and critical for any modern workplace.

John Stepper, in his book, "Working Out Loud: Building a Better Career and Life" https://workingoutloud.com/en/about describes this skill as 'working out loud'. It is a way of building relationships through the spirit of co-operation and collaboration that is brought about by making your work visible to others.

In recent years, our tools and technology such as Yammer and Microsoft Teams as well as the sharing functions of many of our Office applications have allowed this to happen. Where team members can collaborate, comment, and ask questions about the work. For example:

- How did your colleague come up with those actions for to align to your company's marketing strategy?
- Why did she use a particular application in Microsoft Teams to streamline a business process and not another method?
- How did he come up with that idea to solve how recruitment can be redesigned when he spoke to his friends who had recently lost their jobs?

What transparent work provides is the thinking and behaviours behind that presentation, document, or process. It goes behind-the-scenes and makes visible the invisible.

To some this is going to be a scary concept after all, it is like Colonel Sanders giving away his secret herbs and spices. However, what you're doing is that you're laying bare the process of your work so that others can learn from it, solve a problem they may have, or it may give them an idea that in turn, they will share to others.

Showing and sharing your work openly and transparently allows for teams to innovate because it allows diversity of ideas, opinions, and perspectives to be out in the open.

The value to your team members is that it enables them to save time searching for information and duplicating work that was undertaken elsewhere.

To your organisation, it leverages and scales your people's ideas across their teams, departments, and organisational boundaries and eventually, saves money for the organisation in the long term because it reduces co-ordination, re-work, and duplication but most importantly, helps you survive, thrive and flourish in a changing environment.

Let's look at some ways to use Microsoft 365 to show and share your work with your company.

Get Cooking!

1. Create a Yammer community around what you learned today: If your organisation has Yammer, set up a Yammer community called "Today I Learned" where community members can share tips, resources, screencasts, videos, and any helpful content around problems that they had in their work

2. Dedicate a Microsoft Teams channel for showing and sharing your work. You can do the same in your respective Microsoft Teams. Set up a channel called "What I am working on", where team members can share tips of how they solved a specific problem or an 'a-ha' moment for that specific team project

3. Create a Show Your Work 30-day campaign on a SharePoint news page: In your organisation, undertake a 30-day campaign encouraging people to show and share their work. Every day share a question or task that encourages people to share and show the thinking behind their work. You can automate these by using PowerAutomate to go to Yammer; or create a SharePoint news page dedicated to showing and sharing your work. Here's some daily ideas to get started with and why not add more of your own?

   a. What's a problem they solved today?

b. What's the best shortcut they learned for PowerPoint?

c. What's a tip they can share for Word?

d. What's a favourite formula they can share for Excel?

e. Post a photo of themselves working from home, office, or laboratory

f. What's something that made them scratch their head today?

g. How did they make someone smile today? (or how did someone make them smile today?)

h. Who helped them out today?

i. Post a photo of you at your work

j. Share a story of how you helped a customer today

k. What's a problem that you're working on today?

l. What would you like to know today?

m. Share how you set up your workspace from home

n. Share your favourite YouTube channels or podcasts that help you with your work.

4. Give a behind the scenes tour of your workspace or work lab using video (uploaded to Yammer or Stream): Using the video camera on your phone, take people on a behind the scenes tour of the

office, workshop, or workspace. You can show people how it is set up; explain why it's set up in that way and interview colleagues about how they work too. People are curious about each other's workspaces so it's a good opportunity to reveal these to your team members. Alternatively, to make things even more interesting, swap departments. That is, have a marketing team member interview the IT department and vice versa. It makes for interesting viewing as they're more likely to ask the questions the audience is thinking. Upload the video to Yammer or Stream where people can also use the comment area for discussion

5. Undertake a Teams or Yammer Live Event in a workplace: Is there something interesting happening in a team department this week? Why not set up a Teams or Yammer Live Event so people can watch this in the process of happening? It could be an activity in a leadership training event; it may be how graduates are preparing a presentation on their program to a senior leader and we watch them discuss, debate, and build their presentation and hear them explain the process of how they're doing this.

FINDING WHAT YOU WANT

Learn more about this skill

"I must emphasize, no matter how obvious it sounds, that good curating depends upon a bottomless passion and curiosity for looking and questioning; and the desire to communicate that excitement"
– Donna De Salvo

Think that you're overwhelmed with information? Well, you are right. By 2025, it is estimated that 463 exabytes will be created each day globally which is equivalent to 212 765 957 DVDs per day (dive deeper into the statistics via: https://www.visualcapitalist.com/what-happens-in-an-internet-minute-in-2019/)

It is mindboggling but is it any wonder that in a world where information is at our fingertips, we are starved of insight, wisdom, and knowledge? This is what is known as the "information paradox" (https://technologyandsociety.org/information-paradox-drowning-in-information-starving-for-knowledge/) and may be attributed to quality being drowned out by quantity and its obsolescent nature.

But how do we overcome this? We need to look at ways where we can find, filter, aggregate, distil, and synthesise information from different credible and relevant information sources that aren't influenced by commercial interests and brands. That means, we need to hone our curation skills so that we can ensure that information that comes to us is relevant, critical, and trusted.

Rohit Bhargava in describes a curator as "someone who continually finds, groups, organises and shares the best and most relevant content on a specific issue online. The most vital component of this job is the word continually." (https://anderspink.com/documents/content-curation-book.pdf)

I like to think that curators are better than Google. Why? Curators can source content from various sources then filter it so that only the most relevant content makes it through. They can add their own value through providing context by a summary, or comment that makes it align to the topic, subject, or organisation. They are also able to share it to the relevant audience at the right time and place. (Ref: https://anderspink.com/documents/content-curation-book.pdf

What this means is that your organisation can harness the power of collective intelligence and stay smart in an ever-changing world. Here's an opportunity to help your employees become curators.

Your teams can share:

1. Industry news and developments
2. Trends and research data
3. Tips and Practices

Let's face it, using Google to search for information on the web can result in an overload of information that we have to trawl through.

One of the key skills of the digital age is being able to search effectively on the web to find what we need, when we need it and in the form that we want it. You may have learned how to use search parameters to filter information or use the settings to home in on attributes that you were looking for.

Microsoft Search, however, does all this for you.

It allows you to search for people, files and more through the programs they're already working in. So, if you're using Microsoft Word or PowerPoint, Microsoft Search allows you to find information without the need of remembering where it is located. For example, you can be working on a PowerPoint presentation and need information that was in a Word document. Using Microsoft Search bar in PowerPoint, you can find this information directly.

Another time saver for searching for information is that if you use Microsoft Bing, you can search for documents, files, and people inside your company in parallel to searching the public internet as well (Intelligent Search for Business with Bing - Microsoft).

Currently there are many different tools and applications outside of the Microsoft ecosphere to help you manage, filter, curate, and sort out content. Some of these applications are also available as integrations and connectors that can be added to your Microsoft programs such as Microsoft Teams to do the searching and filtering for you.

If you're interested to explore a few of these then here are some that you can start with and add to your Microsoft Team channels:

1. Feedly: Feedly is a news aggregator that compiles news feeds from a variety of online sources. You can customise the search terms, create boards and have information filtered so that it blocks out certain terms and conditions. See www.feedly.com

2. Wakelet: Wakelet is another aggregating tool that allows you to save, organise, and share content from across the web in collections that you can keep private or ones in which you can collaborate on with others or even make public. Wakelet is a powerful tool that allows you to curate content (photos, videos, social media posts, links, documents and more) in a way that tells a story.

You can create different resources such as content libraries, FAQ documents, project portfolios, newsletters and guidebooks and then integrate and embed these Wakelet boards into Microsoft Teams and Microsoft OneNote. See www.wakelet.com

But what about some Microsoft products to assist with curation? Here are some to consider:

3. RSS Feeds: RSS stands for "Really Simple Syndication". Websites are changing information constantly and as such, if we were to check on each of these websites individually for updated information, it will take a great chunk out of our day. Instead, we can use RSS Feeders that do this on our behalf. RSS has been around for many years, and you may have been using it already in Microsoft Outlook to stream updates of your favourite websites into your email inbox. You can now do the same thing in Microsoft Teams and SharePoint.

4. Microsoft Edge Collections: This new function in the Microsoft Edge browser is a great tool that allows you to create collections of bookmarks. What sets Edge Collections apart from a standard Bookmark Manager is that you can add your own value to these collections by way of commentary and context through an Edge note. You can create collections on assorted topics, add your commentary then export to Word or Excel. Business applications include creation of resources guides such as training workbooks, induction guides and on-the-job performance support especially if you want people to refer to specific sites. Learn more at: https://support.microsoft.com/en-au/help/4558542/organize-your-ideas-with-collections-in-microsoft-edge

A word about Microsoft Viva

At the time of drafting this book, Microsoft Viva was still new to the market as Microsoft's new Employment Experience platform. We anticipate that it will make an impact in how people access communication, knowledge, learning, resources, insights, and networks in their organisation. It will enable people to access and harness knowledge across the organisation through artificial intelligence.

Microsoft Viva will make sense of organisational data through harnessing the collective knowledge and expertise so that people can find each other and put their respective knowledge, skills, and experience to work together. It filters, creates, and curates topics, projects, and people to create knowledge centres thus saving time and effort to search for information and people.

Microsoft Viva, however, should not replace the need for sense-making and contextualising for problem solving, valued decision-making and building team insights. This is still very much a human skill.

Get Cooking:

1. Create your own Microsoft Edge Collection on a topic or business interest of your own choice related to a project you are working on. Add notes to each of the sites and export that collection to a Word document to create a resource from it. Alternatively, share the Collections link to your Teams channel and encourage others to do the same so that you can have a conversation on the best content that supports your project.

2. Set up a Wakelet Board: Use this content curation platform to curate your references (or curate

collectively). You can then add this app as a tab in your Microsoft Teams channel. Your imagination is the only limit here. At Adopt & Embrace we used Wakelet to create team learning plans to upskill ourselves in MS PowerAutomate and place this into our Power Platform Training Teams Channel.

3. Add an RSS Connector to your Teams Channel. In Teams > Apps> Search for RSS and select the Team and channel you want to connect it to. The connector will send periodic updates from the address that you want to receive updates from. For example, we have a Teams channel dedicated to all Microsoft 365 updates. These updates are automatically fed into the channel and accessible by everyone. For more information on how to do this refer to: https://docs.microsoft.com/en-us/MicrosoftTeams/office-365-custom-connectors

4. Add an RSS Connector to Your Teams Channel: an alternative way of doing the above is simply to use the PowerAutomate template. https://flow.microsoft.com/en-us/galleries/public/templates/2ec391a0360311e78d1a71a4a5053b4e/post-message-on-teams-when-a-

rss-feed-is-published/

5. Explore Microsoft Viva
   https://www.microsoft.com/en-au/microsoft-viva

6. Use PowerAutomate to curate tweets with certain hashtags. Ever see tweets in Twitter that you want to capture, retweet, and then collect because they have valuable information that you can use for a project? You can easily do this with PowerAutomate templates. For example, create your own specific hashtag such as *#GreatIdeaForOurTeam* then set up an automation that siphons tweets that you include this hashtag directly into a Teams channel or tab.

   a. Use this flow template:
      https://us.flow.microsoft.com/en-us/galleries/public/templates/7200cd7035fe11e78d1a71a4a5053b4e/post-on-microsoft-teams-when-a-new-tweet-matches-the-specified-hashtag/

   b. Why not go wider and share those great ideas not just with your team but with your organisation in Yammer as well? Use this flow template https://us.flow.microsoft.com/en-us/galleries/public/templates/318e08a4dba9 4d3fa948678696eb1408/post-to-yammer-if-a-new-tweet-appears-with-the-specified-hashtag/

c. Use PowerAutomate to curate tweets to Microsoft Planner boards: For example, if you want to set up learning plans for your team and come across great content for them to read, listen to, watch, and explore, create your own hashtag, and automate those to go directly to a Microsoft Planner board from where you can share to your team members. It is a terrific way to create a collection of links to learning resources. You can then add these Planner boards as tabs in your relevant Teams channels.

EFFECTIVE NOTETAKING

Learn more about this skill

*"Very often, gleams of light come in a few minutes'
sleeplessness, in a second perhaps; you must fix them. To
entrust them to the relaxed brain is like writing on water;
there is every chance that on the morrow there will be no
slightest trace left of any happening."*
– Antonin Sertillanges

On Level 4 in the State Library of Victoria in
Melbourne, Australia, is the Dome Gallery. Once
you stop and admire the view below of the Latrobe
Reading Room, take a wander through the exhibition
called the World of the Book. I have lost count how
many times I have seen this exhibition. The World of
the Book exhibition covers aspects of book design,
production, and illustration from the Middle Ages to
today.

What I loved about this exhibition was taking my
time to ponder over the notebooks – the ideas scribbled

by curious authors, scientists, and artists into journals **before** their ideas were published into books.

It is as if I was privy to their thoughts at that moment in time. The time before the true inspiration struck that set them down a path to make the creation – the book or the illustration that we know so well today.

In a cupboard in my home office, I have a stack of old Spirax A4 ring binders. Each one labelled with the year and within each one, a complete mess of handwritten notes from long forgotten team meetings. I run my hand over the indented paper made by a scratchy Bic pen and read about the ideas I came up with then. Once again, I'm given an opportunity to return to a time and place to revisit my thoughts which would otherwise have been lost and forgotten.

I am a witness to my messy thinking.

Today, my note taking is slightly different. The paper has made way for online but where is my messy thinking located today?

Where in the past, I had clippings, post it notes and fluro highlighted pages summarised what I found in my own words to create my own sense of what I found and read; now I am a digital hoarder of web links to articles, resources, infographics, websites, podcasts and more that sit scattered across bookmark collections, in online note books, on mobile phone apps, on book readers such as Kindle and on my devices.

Lots of bookmarks but precious little note taking.

Have we become digital hoarders and lost the art of taking notes?

Why take notes anyway? Who has time for that?

Taking effective notes enables us to take a more focussed approach to our work. It allows us to uncover patterns and connections in the world around us and then identify contradicting information. Note taking allows us to put our brain on paper – or on screen – so that we can make sense of it, define it, and structure it.

At a time when we have a variety of tools that can help us capture information in different ways such as book notes, handwritten notes, screenshots, photos, videos, audio files, and web pages, we need a place for us to make sense of these all and create a system where we see the links between them to gain insights and improve our thinking.

It is easy to let go of this critical activity to focus more on DOING your work however, for us to become better knowledge workers, we need to be THINKING about our work too and creating innovative ideas for our future.

That is where sharpening our skill for effective note taking (in whatever format) will help us.

Get Cooking!

1. Create a Collaborative Notebook for each of your team projects using OneNote. Each of us takes notes differently so rather than adopting a "same way/one way" approach in these notebooks, consider using OneNote how educators use it – a space for classroom collaboration and an individual space for each student. You can use the same concept for your teamwork. In your team collaborative notebooks, consider setting up the tabs to allow for specific areas of project-based collaboration vs personal note taking to allow people to use their own note taking system without risking losing their ideas into other notebooks and applications

2. Consider running a professional development session with your work team on how to take effective and systematic digital notes all of which can be incorporated into OneNote. Many of these can be done in diverse ways and if you have a Surface Pro and pen (or an iPad with a stylus), you also can incorporate more visual and creative elements to your notetaking. For example, you can investigate different ways to take notes such as

mind mapping, sketch noting or bullet journaling

3. Create your own template for Microsoft OneNote that is specific to your individual or team note taking needs (Create or customize page templates (microsoft.com)). OneNote comes with a variety of different pre-designed Page Templates that you can use. By creating your own, you're more likely to enjoy OneNote because it aligns with your personal preferences for taking notes

4. Create a Curiosity Notebook in Microsoft OneNote and encourage people to share ONE thing they learned that day. It can be shared in the form of a note; a drawing; a video; sketch note anything. This could be something they've observed at work or their work project. Over time, there will be a collection of notes from everyone where people can see patterns, connections, and links. It also hones your team's observational skills when they are required to write down their "curious moments" of the day

5. Get into the habit of tagging your notes so that you can filter them in future (Apply a tag to a note in OneNote (microsoft.com)). OneNote tags have different applications such as tracking items and

managing your workflow or assigning and managing the work of your team. OneNote has a variety of tags such as:

a. Ideas
b. Movie to see
c. Book to Read
d. Discuss with <Person A>
e. Important
f. Question
g. Critical
h. To Do
i. Remember for Later
j. And many more (and you can add more of your own)

These tags serve as 'information reminders' that you can then search for and filter to create a Tags summary.

MAKING SENSE OF COMPLEXITY

Learn more about this skill

"I would rather have questions that can't be answered than answers that can't be questioned."
– Richard Feynman

At the time of writing this chapter, MasterChef Australia was on our televisions in the evenings.

It was a battle between previous MasterChef winners trying to prepare and present the best meal out of the ingredients and recipes provided under the added pressure of an allocated time to complete the task. Meanwhile, they had to deal with all sorts of obstacles that would arise such as having to recreate a dish without an essential ingredient; using the kitchen appliances and tools they had around them in novel ways; pesky judges butting in the middle of their preparation to ask probing questions that left them

171

uncertain and anxious and their peers yelling encouragement from above.

I admired each of the chefs for having to deal with a high-pressure environment where they didn't know what to expect in each of the challenges. It made me realise that this is how modern workers are working every day, having to deal with complex situations that are changing by the day or by the hour. The way they used to do business can be interrupted or become obsolete, and they are scrounging around for best practices when there are none – especially when our entire organisational systems aren't stable anymore.

According to Cynefin, a sensemaking framework devised by David Snowden (https://en.wikipedia.org/wiki/Cynefin_framework) there are five decision-making domains called Simple, Complicated, Complex, Chaotic, and Disorder, that offer a place from which behaviours can be analysed and decisions made. The domain of Complex represents 'unknown unknowns' which is where our systems and society seems to be in a place now. That is, a situation that is not fully knowable and not fully predictable. (https://www.frontrowagile.com/blog/posts/82-navigating-complexity-aka-cynefin-for-dummies)

In such situations, the only way we can navigate through this phase where our actions are constantly changing the situation and environment, is to probe, sense, and respond. We need to be in continual feedback loops where we make an assessment for the next step to undertake. This will allow for emergent work practices and new behaviours to unfold that will help our people and their teams.

But how do we create a sense of place from which to analyse our behaviours and make decisions especially when everything seems to be unordered, and we only have the benefit of hindsight?

It will require each of us to ask questions about how and the way we work individually and collectively.

Here are some activities to get you started – to probe, to make sense and to respond – with navigating complexity using the ingredients of Microsoft 365 (which coincidentally, may change)!

Get Cooking:

1. Create a Microsoft Teams Channel where Team members write a daily post: Allocate five minutes at the end of the day to write a reflective post about what you learned today how it helped or hindered you in your work. These daily blog posts capture the moments in your day on certain projects. If you are on different projects, share your thoughts across the different teams. They need not be War and Peace. Over time, with others in your team adding their thoughts, you will see how the collective thinking and emotions are reflected and visible through the life of the project

2. Create a OneNote notebook where every team member has a section of their own to blog or post ideas around a question that is posed to the team: For every project in your team, why not have a OneNote notebook where there are sections for collaboration but also sections for individual team members where they can use as a 'dumpster' of their ideas, scribbles, quotes, audio and video notes, photos and links related to that project and a question posed to that team every week?

3. Use Whiteboarding App in your Team Meetings: Use the whiteboarding app in your team meetings to ask questions and enable group brainstorming activities. Your team members can use the online post it notes or the pen tools to create mind maps to capture all ideas and possibilities

4. Use Whiteboard, OneNote, or a specialist Mind mapping tool: Whichever you select, add it to your channel in Microsoft Teams as a Tab for collaborative mind mapping

5. Create a Probe Bot: Okay, that doesn't sound right, but hear me out. Using Power Apps, or Power Virtual Agents, build a bot that can be added to your project team that sends out questions on rotation every week in your Team Channel that

encourages people to stop and think about the work they're doing so that they can make sense of it and jot down some quick responses. Some questions to use can be:

a. Why are you doing it this way?
b. What can you do differently today?
c. How would you explain what you do to a child?
d. What experiment can you do today?
e. What if you swapped something out today and replaced it with something else?
f. Has your idea been done before?
g. What's something you can improve on your work today?
h. What's a new habit you can start doing from today?

6. Create Communities of Innovation in Yammer: These are communities consisting of people who come from various parts of the organisation and backgrounds (or External Groups) who come together for the purposes of solving problems through testing, experiments, breaking apart and hacking, and proposing alternatives. Their nature is such that they are short-term, smaller in size, and focused on a specific question. These communities probe, provoke, reframe, and

experiment. Participation in these communities where you are collaborating and co-creating creative and innovative solutions can also be seen as professional and personal development and where an organisation can use the ideas for new products and services and identify participants for new roles and opportunities. Learn more at https://en.wikipedia.org/wiki/Communities_of_inn ovation

BUILDING CONNECTION THROUGH CREATIVITY

Learn more about this skill

"Creativity involves breaking out of established patterns in order to look at things in a different way."
– Edward de Bono

I have been an avid user of Twitter for many years, building up a global network of people across my various interests and fields of endeavours in learning and development, technology, history, education, and many more. One of the things I noticed during the time of pandemic is that my network, many of whom shared only tweets and posts about their work or their field, were now sharing more photos and videos of their lives.

Some shared their artworks they were creating such as sketches, music, paintings, and other creations. Others were sharing photos of sunsets and sunrises; their gardens; the fruit and vegetables they were growing in their gardens; or the books they were reading.

Suddenly, the people who I knew as the experts in their field seemed to me to be more human, more real. They were showing more of their authentic self in these social networks and now broadened the conversation beyond work and productivity.

People were now taking the time to rediscover something they had lost or overlooked: creative pursuits as well as learning new skills because they had unstructured time to be able to explore creative pursuits as a means of sensemaking.

Jane Hart, founder of the Centre for Modern Workplace (https://www.modernworkplacelearning.com/cild/) and I also created a website Discover2Learn – https://discover2learn.com/ where we curated different ways for people to use their time during pandemic lockdowns to be curious, explore, discover new things, have fun, and learn.

It has long been accepted that at times of stress and trauma artists produce their best work. Shakespeare wrote King Lear during times of plague and Sir Isaac Newton came up with his theory of gravity… but before you become disheartened because you've lost the motivation to do anything at all right now, we would say "don't beat yourself up over this." We are going through one of the toughest times in our lives and we are all making sense of it differently and in our own time.

The determining factor for creativity is not vast output of work you produce – but what you don't. It is not about how many sketches you draw, how progressed you are into the new language you're learning, or how many words you wrote in that best seller novel you're writing.

What you are doing instead is focussing on undertaking pursuits that make meaning for you. It means you're investing your time to reconsider, rebuild, and understand a new reality. If you're not feeling creative, then that's okay because you're deep into the heart of processing and these things take time.

You'll know when you're ready.

So how can we bring out moments of creativity in our work? Well, we can't force this to happen. Creativity is the "use of imagination or original ideas to create something". What we can do is to enable situations and allow time for people to let their minds wander, have the space to create, and just be themselves without judgement.

Get Cooking:

1. Incorporate a creative and interactive fun activity each MS Teams meeting: This might mean rather than starting the work immediately, take the time

to incorporate something that will break the ice and get the participants ready for the meeting. There are a variety of different articles on the internet with many ideas for what you can do here. Maybe just start with "What is your biggest personal win or professional win from the past week?"

2. Encourage team members to create their own video or audio content: If you have people who are keen videographers or photographers; or people who have their own podcasts out of work hours, why not encourage them to put their skills to use for workplace contexts? Create your own Microsoft Stream channel or workplace podcasts and share that with others in your organisation. Not only do they put their skills into practice, but they're also showcasing and promoting your team and its' great work across the organisation

3. Explore the myriad of Icebreakers and Teams Activities you can do during your MS Teams meetings: We have been curating a variety of articles and posts online on how to undertake ice breakers and team building virtually. Check them out here:
    https://wakelet.com/wake/c3LMOjpmbTi2c1UsX7i

4. Create your own Live Event Show: Using Microsoft Teams Live Events, stream your own team-based channel related to any topic that can be work or leisure related

5. Conduct Social Activities: Our team did online trivia nights for our staff and their families as well as virtual tours of our neighbourhoods as ways of getting to know each other

6. Use Yammer Communities: Create interest communities such as pets, music, food, and books and anything else you can think of that would enable people to share content such as photos and videos of their interests and creations to others

7. Create your own Lip Dub with your team: A lip dub is a wonderful team activity where you can choose the music and capture videos of your team lip synching to the words. All it requires is someone to pull together the video files and add the music to create a co-created video that captures the sentiment of the team going through this time in history.

BUILDING & PARTICIPATING IN COMMUNITIES

Learn more about this skill

"I alone cannot change the world, but I can cast a stone across the waters to create many ripples."
– Mother Teresa

Every couple of years, my parents and I take a week-long trip into regional Victoria (Australia) where we visit the historical towns and sights of our state. We stop off at vineyards, cheese factories, farms, and pubs to enjoy the local produce these places have to offer. Driving into every town, I used to see the old buildings on the main street that claimed they were a Mechanics Institute. This made me curious because I'd see them in every town, so I set off on trying to understand their history.

The Mechanics Institutes were the pre-cursor to national libraries and technical colleges. Founded in Scotland in the early 1800s by Jason Birkbeck, they were created to train and skill up the labourers (many who were illiterate) to become factory workers for the Industrial Revolution. The institutes were so popular in their day that quickly, many towns across the UK, Australia, and America soon held free public lectures in arts, sciences, and technology to help the community progress and be ready for industrialisation.

But what do Mechanics Institutes have to do with communities?

At a time when we see our world at the crux of societal change, you must wonder if building, participating, and engaging in communities (whether they're online or not) are the new "institutes?"

That is, where do our people find the means to understand what knowledge, skills, and capabilities they need to flourish in a new world of work especially when our educational systems and institutions are also going through this transformation?

Are communities now the places where we learn and create new knowledge and in doing so become ready for a new world?

Managers and leaders now have an opportunity to see the value of communities that are built and created inside their organisation (as well as outside) as places where their people can gather and share knowledge and perspectives that brings value back to their work.

A workplace without active communities, is a workplace devoid of ideas and insights, where the authoritative voice drowns out employees learning from and with each other.

What can we do to encourage people to build, participate and engage in communities at work and outside of work? Here are some activities to get you started.

Get Cooking!

1. Encourage the use of enterprise social networks such as Yammer to create and engage in communities. Encourage people to ask questions, show and share their work, and participate in online discussions as part of their daily workflow. See the use of Yammer and any other enterprise social network as an integral part of your team member's work

2. Build specific community management and community building skills into your team's professional development plans. Encourage and support the champions who help others to use and share their voice through online communities

3. Participate in your organisation's Yammer using your own voice, stories, and experiences (don't have others post on your behalf)

4. Create an online community around a workplace event or program which will ensure conversations and networking happens before, during and after these

5. Encourage your team members to be members of external communities (eg. Microsoft Technical Communities or external Yammer Groups) so that they can build their skills, capabilities and networks in their specific expertise area

6. Consider joining our own Rapid Circle Adopt & Embrace Academy, a community of adoption, change and learning peers around the world who value knowledge, experience, and resource sharing on all aspects of workplace transformation with M365 www.adoptandembrace.academy

CONTINUOUS
LEARNING & DEVELOPMENT

Learn more about this skill

"The capacity to learn is a gift, the ability to learn is a skill,
the willingness to learn is a choice"
– Brian Herbert

The global pandemic provided an instant wake up call to many organisations as they scrambled to support their employees to work from home. It exposed glaring problems with departments as they needed to train their people to use the tools and technology, systems, and applications in a fleeting time frame and without the luxury of structured and staggered roll outs with defined change management and training programs. It was a baptism of fire when it came to upskilling entire workforces across national and international boundaries in what seemed to be, overnight.

As someone who has been in the field of learning and development for many years, part of me felt that this was what was needed to have organisations sit up and take note that indeed, we had to change our thinking when it came to the importance of continual learning and development. The pandemic provided the trigger to jolt us out of our comfort zones and expose our flaws in current thinking. We had to get comfortable with not knowing everything. We had to relearn.

Pre-covid, we were seeing the signs of constant change and demand in our workplaces. Whole industries, business processes, and practices were being disrupted by massive changes in customer supply and demand globally which changed our business models. We were seeing this impact to our daily work. It seemed that every day something was always changing; we were in constant back-to-back meetings; our inbox was out of control; we couldn't find the information we were looking for when we needed it; the left hand didn't know what the right hand was doing; there was little breathing space room to plan, question, reflect before jumping into the next project.

Something had to give.

The pandemic caused an initial flurry of activity to move our work online however, surprisingly over time when this activity died down, it began to offer us some space for us to question why – and how – we were doing things. After many organisations skilled up their people to use Microsoft Teams and OneDrive, their focus turned to how they can put their experiences into other uses such as learning and development.

In our work, we saw this through the variety of different industries who began to approach us for support and assistance. It wasn't our usual customer industry. Instead, people from training departments in medium and corporate organisations; small business vendors who wanted to move their facilitator-led training online through to educators across primary, secondary, and tertiary institutions began to see the value of blended learning were approaching us.

In later parts of this book, we will explore the different recipes for how to use Microsoft 365 as a learning tool for educators and training departments however, in this chapter, we will turn our focus to the importance of a skill that we will all need to flourish in a future world – and that is, continual and lifelong learning.

Why Learn and Why Now?

Alvin Toffler once said, 'The illiterate of the 21st century will not be those who cannot read and write, but those who cannot learn, unlearn, and relearn.' Learning is essential to our existence and ensures our survival.

But how can organisations help their people to learn how to learn? How can they prepare them for a world of constant disruption? How can they use the Microsoft 365 tools at their fingertips to build new behaviours and workplace practices?

As well as using the topics in this chapter to get started (after all, this chapter IS about learning skills needed for a new world of work), here are some additional considerations for you:

Cultivate curiosity and a growth mindset

Psychologist Carol S. Dweck pioneered the growth mindset where "people believe that their most basic abilities can be developed through dedication and hard work – brains and talent are just the starting point." The growth mindset creates the resilience needed for accomplishing goals and a love of learning.

Managers and team leaders can look at supporting their people to build more question and reflection time into their work. Alternatively, they can allow time for their team members to work on side projects or stretch assignment that build new skills and capabilities. However, it's not just enabling the curiosity and growth mindset of their people, managers can also ask what their people are learning. For example:

- What did they learn from reading that book?
- What themes came out that can be applied in their work when they watched that video?
- What experiences outside of work have they learned that can be applied in work?
- What are they studying outside of work that has direct or indirect relevance and meaning to their job?

Focus on building capabilities not competence

The world of work is changing fast, and it is impossible to keep up with the paces of change and the various tools, technology, programs, new business models and industries.

You may have heard about competency and capability but when would you use one over the other aren't they the same?

In today's world, the words differ because as Simon Terry explains in his blog post, Competency or Capability: Mindsets Matter.

(https://simonterry.tumblr.com/post/62886098082/com petency-or-capability-mindsets-matter)

Competency is the possession of the required skills, knowledge, and capacity to do a job today while capability is about the qualities and the potential to be developed.

Many organisations who have focussed on building competence frameworks for specific job roles have now realised that these are now redundant because they are out of date. Instead, they have turned their focus to building employee capabilities which are likely to be more successful to help the organisation navigate and manage change easily.

Get comfortable with data

It is now easier than ever to have at our disposal a wealth of data from our organisations that make us better decision makers. Rather than making guesses to what we believe our people need by way of their learning and development; we can look at the data – usually provided by visually immersive and interactive insights such as those in Power BI to establish where the gaps are and what steps to take next. Alternatively, at an individual level, Viva Insights provide anyone with a wealth of information that will enable them to personalise and customise their own time, attention, focus and networks to close performance and skill gaps.

Incorporate Experiential Learning Through Work

Experiential learning means learning through immersive experiences. Our work can be seen as a "learning experience" especially if it requires us to solve problems, collaborate and co-operate with others to identify new products, insights, and possibilities. Immersive learning means that workers are building and creating new knowledge that comes from active participation in team project work, testing, trialling, and experimenting on aspects of the work.

One way we will be seeing more of immersive learning environments will be the use of SharePoint Spaces which are immersive and engaging mixed reality experiences (SharePoint spaces (microsoft.com)). With 360-degree videos and mixed reality, teams will be able to build workplace and laboratory experiences that are close to as real life as possible.

Get Cooking:

1. Make time for learning every day. Using Viva Insights, book focus time into your diary every day for 5-10 minutes every day and stick with it! (Alternatively, why not set up a PowerAutomate button alert to block out the next hour in your diary

to focus on your learning?) Here's the template you can use:
https://australia.flow.microsoft.com/en-us/galleries/public/templates/857a9d1ff3204aa2896995776121a743/block-out-my-office-365-calendar-for-an-hour/

2. Browse through the many courses available via Viva Learning and take one. If you liked the course and can see applications to a project team, why not share that course to that relevant Microsoft Teams team and also click Recommend so you can recommend it to specific team members

3. Create your own Personal Learning Plan board in Microsoft Planner. Build out a board where you can add Learning Tasks that you can schedule at various times. Alternatively, create a different board for specific tasks such as "Articles to Read"; "Podcasts to Listen To"; "Books to Read" and "Courses to Attend" and use the note section of the board to capture your learning. To read more about how I use Microsoft Planner to build out a Personal Learning Plan, refer to Create Your Own Learning Play List

https://activatelearning.com.au/2019/11/create-your-learning-playlist/

4. Create a 30-day Learning Campaign on Yammer or through an automated email campaign using

PowerAutomate to send spaced messages to specific target audiences in your company

5. Create Communities of Practice on Yammer Communities. Wenger-Traynor defines Communities of Practice as "groups of people who share a concern or a passion for something they do and learn how to do it better as they interact regularly"

   (https://wenger-trayner.com/resources/what-is-a-community-of-practice/).
   By creating spaces where people can be brought together for collective learning will not only build their skills, capabilities and networks but will also assist the organisation to identify potential new talent

6. Encourage people to share a learning tip every day. This could be through a Yammer Community called 'Today I Learned', through an individual channel in Microsoft Team projects, or as an opening conversation at your next team meeting

7. Encourage participation and contribution in communities such as the Microsoft Technical Communities https://techcommunity.microsoft.com/ Managers can help support staff by building in community contribution and engagement as part of their

employees' learning development plans. Community participation MUST be seen as part of the workflow and an extension to their employees' work, given it is professional development activity

8. Access LinkedIn Learning to undertake a variety of courses. Many organisations already have LinkedIn Learning subscriptions. Alternatively, you may not be aware that many public libraries offer this service for free (sometimes known as Lynda.com) as part of their membership. Check with your local library to see if you can access these courses for free

9. Build your own Learning Path in MS Learn, Microsoft's learning management system with access to certifications, courses, and learning paths customised to your role and interests https://docs.microsoft.com/en-us/learn/

EMPATHY, RESILIENCE & WELLBEING

Learn more about this skill

"Overwork is repulsive to human nature-not work"
– Pyotr Kropotkin

At the time of writing this chapter, I am sitting at my kitchen table on a grey cold Melbourne day. It is Day 41 of Lockdown Version 2.0 as I call it. It is the second time our state has gone into lockdown and this time, with 400,000 additional jobs lost, an 8pm curfew, mandatory wearing of face masks, limits of one hour to be allowed outside for exercise and only one person from each household to visit the supermarket, the lockdown has affected me mentally and emotionally.

I have days of highs and lows. Days where I cry, others where I get angry for no reason at all.

The first lockdown seemed easier despite the initial angst of uncertainty. While others were scrambled to get their business online, I could breathe a sigh of relief.

Virtual and remote work was not new for me as I had been doing it for some years. It also seemed that the whole world was going through this together. There was solidarity as we collectively tried to make sense of this new world. Business scrambled to get their workforce online, teachers pulled together their curriculum to have it delivered virtually, households organised themselves to be able to live, work, and study together under the same roof.

However, the second lock down was different.

For us in Melbourne, it took us by surprise especially when we were going so well keeping the COVID cases down through a major testing program. Imagine our frustration when the numbers started becoming out of control and our premier put a stricter lockdown measure in place to contain the spread of the virus. Meanwhile in other states, restrictions lessened, and their lives returned to some semblance of normality.

But why am I writing this when we all have experienced the effects of this pandemic?

The first time around my colleagues and I were in that "jail cell" together. The second time it felt like I returned to that jail cell only to have the door slammed shut and look out to the world through bars.

I saw my colleagues enjoying long weekends away, working from co-working spaces, and gathering at meals at cafes. It seemed life had gone back to normal for them. In other circumstances, this wouldn't have made an impact on me – after all, they live and work in another state.

However, why was it different this time?

It wasn't jealousy. It was more of a realisation of the injustice of inequality of the situation that was beyond my control (or let's face it, the "perceived inequality" in my head). It felt that these freedoms were denied to me simply because I was in Melbourne: "the leper colony".

I started to think: Is this what people who come from different racial backgrounds feel like? Is this how people who are dispossessed from others in society feel?

The situation showed me that at times, we take our own situations for granted and assume that everyone else is going through the same thing as we are; and dealing with it in the same way – and that this wrong thinking.

The pandemic brought out a situation that many people never imagined. It brought to light the inequalities within our society, but it also blasted some of our own misconceptions when it comes to things such as access to technology and the high-speed internet, working spaces within the home and our own questions about how we work, why we work in the ways we do, and how we could do better to support ourselves and our team members.

Astute companies realised that their team members needed support at this time, and they provided this in various ways.

Some allowed their employees to take time and provide the space so that they could determine a new working pattern that fitted with their family commitments.

Others used their employee assistance programs to provide resources and support networks that their teams could access. Meanwhile managers and teams checked-in with each other to ensure that people did not feel alone or isolated.

While these initiatives supported the employees, questions were also being asked about how the current team and work structures were helping or hindering the mental health and wellbeing of team members. Undoubtedly your own teams may have been asking:

"Should we still have one-hour back-to-back meetings like we did in the office?"

"Should we have private conversations about the project we are working on?"

"Why am I creating this 60-page PowerPoint slide report that no one will read or use?"

Thinking critically about the way we worked changed our perspective when we realised that just because we were always doing our work in one way, doesn't mean that it will serve us in the new world especially when we have seen that peoples' circumstances are all different.

Suddenly, we had to think of new ways of working that did not add additional stress for our team members, but instead, helped them to maintain a sense of balance.

We had to empathise with our fellow colleagues and build in new ways of working that helped not only their resilience to the situation but supported their mental health and wellbeing through this uncertain time.

The effects of the pandemic will be felt for a long time and it's safe to say that we can say goodbye to some of the traditional work practices that may have taken place in an office between 9am and 5pm and which kept our personal situations and work preferences hidden from others.

So, what can we do to help our teams build resilience in the face of change, build empathy when their team members and nurture their health, mental and physical wellbeing? Here are some to start off with.

Get Cooking:

1. Conduct daily check-ins with your teams: Encourage everyone to post how they are doing, ask them to reply to a post you start, or if you are technically minded, create a bot that can sit in your Microsoft Teams channel that sends out an alert every morning that checks in how you're feeling. Alternatively, you can create this in Microsoft Forms as a poll and then automate this to be sent out to your team through email or Team Channels using PowerAutomate

2. Download and use an Employee Check-In App: Why not download and use an employee check-in app already made on Power Apps from the Microsoft Community: https://powerusers.microsoft.com/t5/Emergency-Response-Gallery/Employee-Wellbeing-Check-In-App/td-p/513843 Or why not create your own in Power Apps?

3. Conduct a Health Challenge: Add an app to your Microsoft Teams and conduct a team health challenge. For example, you can use something like Health Hero that allows everyone to connect to their favourite health app or fitness device and rank each other's progress on a leader board. Or encourage people to post screenshots of their Strava wins for

4. Give Thanks, Praise or Kudos: Has someone helped you with a question or challenge this week? Encourage people to openly thank people who have helped them and how. For example, within Microsoft Teams and Yammer, there is a Praise function. Simply click on that and share the love! Alternatively, you can use many of the third-party applications in the App Store in Microsoft Teams to download and add this functionality such as Kudos, Recognize and Hi5. Never underestimate the power of acknowledging people with a thank you

5. Adopt a Buddy System: We used the Icebreaker Bot in MS Teams. Icebreaker would create random connections every week for two people to connect with each other so that they could go out for coffee. Although this bot was designed for icebreakers, you can use the same principle for creating one to find your buddy and to set up virtual meetups or coffee dates

6. Conduct a Weekly Wind Down Meetup in MS Teams: At the end of the week, why not catch up with your team buddies socially? Use it as an opportunity to reflect on the week, in particular:
    a. How did my/our work help or hinder me/us this week?

b. What are three good things our team did this week?
c. What is one professional win and one personal in for me this week?
d. What am I planning or looking forward to over the next week? Tonight? Weekend?

7. Create a Health and Wellbeing Checklist: Using Microsoft List, create a list with all different activities that have been co-created with your team that they can do individually or together. Every week, keep yourselves accountable by making sure you've done one thing on that list that supported your mental health and wellbeing

8. Create your Microsoft Stream Channel on Health and Wellbeing: Using Microsoft Stream, encourage people to share their stories whether in audio or video form about what they're doing for their health, mental and physical wellbeing. If you have avid team members who are yoga instructors or meditation coaches, or fitness gurus outside of work, have them conduct a class on video and share on   Stream

9. Conduct a Weekly Mindfulness Moment in Microsoft Teams: our team conducts regular weekly 15-minute virtual mindfulness moments where we talk and share what has been on our mind regarding

our health and wellbeing for that week. Let the conversation flow with no specified agenda as the topics usually come out in the conversation and people are giving each other ideas and support. In our mindfulness moments we have talked about:

a. How do we manage our time and boundaries?
b. How do we manage stress and anxiety?
c. What apps and tools do we use for meditation?
d. What are we eating and health regimes we are undertaking?
e. How are we reducing our caffeine intake?
f. What are some good breathing exercises?
g. Who's our favourite YouTuber or website for exercise?
h. What creative and sporting pursuits that we are undertaking to give our mind a mental break?

INCLUSIVE WORK PRACTICES & BEHAVIOURS

"Diversity is being invited to the party; inclusion is being asked to dance." – Verna Myers

Learn more about this skill

I watched my sister-in-law try to settle my young six-year-old nephew to sit still and concentrate on his reading activity and I could feel her exasperation and frustration over the Skype call.

"I've had to take leave to do his home schooling. There is simply no way I can work full-time, look after him and home school him plus do all the other jobs around the house during this lockdown. I'm tired. I'm exhausted. I'm over it already!" she cried out.

Meanwhile chatting with other friends who were also thrown into working from home brought on by the pandemic, there were mixed reactions. Some welcomed the opportunity as they didn't have to commute for work; others weren't so happy because it brought up situations where their home – and private lives and situations – were discussed or on view to others.

Where the physical office was a place where we could hide in plain sight from our colleagues and follow the norms expected of us; oddly working from home opened aspects of our private lives. Now, people could see into our homes and spaces, meet our family members and our pet, and peer onto our bookshelves behind us. It brought a disparity which was unexpected. People's living conditions and home situations could now be seen and heard, and it showed us that we were all different.

As I thought about my sister-in-law and while I watched my colleagues juggle home schooling around work and life commitments, I started to wonder about the inequality of working from home for some people.

Is there a correlation between the effectiveness of working from home against people who come from minority backgrounds, poor backgrounds who may not have dedicated spaces in their homes or access to technology to work effectively?

What about the caregivers, many of whom are women – is working from home of value to them?

Or were we seeing another example of bias where flexible work only suiting people who have the means, the technology, access, space, and time for it?

In the Harvard Business Review article, 'Why WFH Isn't Necessarily Good for Women' https://hbr.org/2020/07/why-wfh-isnt-necessarily-good-for-women, it sets out the premise that working from home may not be the "big equaliser for women" because of the research that suggests that it increases work and family conflict and where "women are more likely to carry out more domestic responsibility while working flexibly, whereas men are more likely to prioritize and expand their work spheres." Similarly, as companies change their models of work to be hybrid, there may be a bias towards those who are present in the office, leaving the women who may be working from home out of important conversations.

This brings up the concept of belonging in the workplace – wherever that workplace happens to be. In the physical office, home, or elsewhere.

For many years, companies have been working on diversity and inclusion policies to ensure that everyone gets an equal voice at work. These are important and critical to the effective functioning of the workplace. Having a diverse workforce means that we are valued for our uniqueness and inclusion means they we can take part in work life however, how to do you engender a feeling of belonging especially in a hybrid model where some people may be in the office, others at home while others working across different time zones or at different times of the day?

According to research by Glint https://www.glintinc.com/blog/why-belonging-is-important-at-work-employee-engagement-and-diversity/ "belonging is a fundamental need for human beings and when employees feel they don't belong, whether experiencing day-to-day pain or special circumstances such as working remotely during a pandemic, it damages their ability to focus and engage. When employees feel a strong sense of belonging at work, they are over six times as likely to bring their best selves to work and do the best work." This sense of belonging then helps in engagement and ultimately organisational success.

To promote belonging at work, especially when people will be undertaking work at different times and spaces, leaders will need to look at how they reframe their diversity and inclusion policies to ensure that everyone not only has a voice but can be included in critical conversations at work – and not those who are simply "present" in the physical spaces.

The pandemic has brought about new considerations for diversity and inclusion especially with regards to the unconscious biases that come into play with using remote technologies such as Microsoft Teams. It is now an opportunity to look at how we interact and engage online with our fellow colleagues and team members and consider work practices that support inclusive behaviours for all people.

Get Cooking:

1. Conduct check-ins with your team using Microsoft Teams meetings and ask the following questions such as:
   a. Are you able to bring your whole self to work?
   b. Do you feel appreciated and valued for who you are and not just what you do?
   c. Do you feel that you belong as part of the team?

2. For team meetings in Microsoft Teams consider doing the following:

   a. Have your team share more about themselves (show their home, important people or animals in their life)
   b. Start off team meetings with, "What's one good thing that happened to you this week personally and professionally?"

c. Conduct an emotional check-in at the start or end of the day, or in team meetings where people can share how they're feeling now. You can use the Microsoft Form templates that are ready made and available in Microsoft Teams that measure employee well-being and daily health check-ins

d. Reduce the length of your meetings

e. Start your meetings at 5 or 10 minutes past the hour to encourage people to take a break, get away from their device, and stretch

f. Have everyone speak at the meeting by asking them direct questions. Pay attention to those who aren't speaking and ensure you acknowledge and credit those who share ideas and insights by using the kudos or 'give thanks' function in Microsoft Teams or Yammer.

3. Ensure you use the accessibility options and insights for your team meetings and live events. For example, you can caption your videos in Microsoft Stream, use the accessibility checker on any Microsoft 365 document as well as use captions in team meetings. For more information, check out the

https://blogs.microsoft.com/accessibility/

4. Consider recording team meetings so that they're available for team members if they cannot attend them personally at that time. For recorded meetings, consider adding additional assistance by time stamping your videos by providing detailed comments under the video so that people can go directly to the relevant topics that were mentioned

5. Before commencing any formal presentations and events, acknowledge the traditional owners of the land. This is typical for Australian and New Zealand and is a way of showing awareness of and respect for the Aboriginal owners of the land on which the meeting or event is being held

6. Microsoft has made available a training module called Unconscious Bias https://www.mslearning.microsoft.com/course/721 69/launch that you can use with your teams to help identify unconscious bias in your work practices.

Now that we have explored some of the important skills that contribute to effective individual and teamwork in your digital workplace, now let's explore some recipes for common scenarios or use cases in your workplace.

PART 3:
RECIPES FOR COMMON USE CASES

If you have made it this far in your chef classes you would now have a deeper knowledge of ingredients, and their properties – as well as some of the skills required to work well with your ingredients.

Take a loaf of bread for example – we know it has a crusty exterior and a soft and fluffy inside. When we serve it up to our customers, we want it to retain its shape and firmness.

This is where our skills come in – in our chef classes we would have learned the way to handle bread and cut it into slices is with a serrated knife. The serrated blade confidently saws through the exterior and through the interior without squashing the bread or ripping it apart. Ever tried doing this with a regular blade that is non-serrated? The blade has trouble cutting through the crust, requiring you to put more of your own force into it, which sometimes won't end well if you're not careful. What else happens is that you end up squashing the bread or tearing it – resulting with a mangled piece of bread with the crust falling off. Not a good day in the kitchen.

The same happens in the workplace when we use the wrong tool for our job at hand, resulting in something short of what we wanted to achieve.

Ever tried to run a project using email? Not fun.

There could be multiple components to your project – each component engaging with stakeholders as well as collaborating with the other components. As the project manager you either; choose to sacrifice yourself by requesting to be cc'ed on every email so you don't miss anything, but die foraging through your email piecing together where things are at. Or you instead keep on track of progress by asking to be updated, which usually results in constantly chasing people for status.

Whichever method – you just seem to be spending too much of your time being a personal assistant to yourself.

So, here's the thing; you're using a regular blade knife, when you need a serrated knife for this type of work practice.

The serrated knife approach requires 'ingredients' that can enable the required 'skills' ("Showing & Sharing Your Work", "Finding What You Want", "Inclusive Work Practices & Behaviours") to bake a great look and tasting 'recipe' (visibility of project work, and the ability to self-serving project progress).

In this case our recommended ingredients may be – Planner for task tracking and accountability, and Team channel conversations for doing the work and visibility to those working on other parts of the project.

Once in this mode it enables a different approach to awareness and progress. The onus is on the project manager to look at all the visible work and self-serve awareness of the latest conversations and task status, and not for the project team members to endlessly ping the manager.

A shift from a push to a pull approach – or perhaps we could say a publish/follow model, rather than a sender/receiver model.

In this case using the right set of apps (ingredients), that enable the right practices (skills) for the right job eg. project visibility (recipe) is the main theme for this section of the book. Only, project visibility is just one type of use case or need – we'll explore many others.

Another slightly related theme we will see is using (cooking) the apps (ingredients) in the *right way* for the job you need done or outcomes you want to achieve (recipe).

I recall once hearing a story on the radio where a mum was teaching her daughter how to cook. At one point the daughter asked her mum why she cut off the ends of her ham before she put it in the pan. Her mother replied that's how her mum taught her. This observation stuck with the mum, so she decided to ask her mum the same question. The grandmother replied that she cut off the ends of the ham so it would fit in her small pan – she didn't have a large enough pan to accommodate the size of the ham.

Now breaking old habits or snapping out of that auto-pilot mode is important here for your recipe to look like the picture in the book, and hopefully taste good as well.

For example, if we decide to shift from broadcast emails to an app like Yammer to communicate to the organisation – we need to break those old habits of "communicating at" our organisation based on our past assumptions of how we got the job done, to having a "conversation with" our organisation.

Carrying over our old model or way of doing things may be a lost opportunity to improve our practices and the quality of our outcomes – or it can even lead to failure. We end up blaming the tool, rather than our lack of forming new approaches and breaking old habits. We miss out on the affordances the new tool can enable. Or as some would say, you failed cause you "didn't get it".

Let's question our mum's cooking method (did I dare just say that?), and let's talk to our grandmother – and then we can decide for ourselves that if we want to achieve a more inclusive culture, enable people to show their talent, and simply engage our staff, then we need to go about things a new way. Sorry, Mum, I'm not going to cut off the ends of the ham today... or hey, maybe I'll just buy a bigger pan.

When you are reading the use cases in this chapter and thinking about your own, keep in mind – "Using the right set of apps, for the right job" and "Using the apps in the right way, for the job you need done"

We hope these use cases inspire you, and trigger ways for you to build your own with your team.

The following chapters really require us to have the purpose-based knowledge and skills to turn these ingredients into the meal that will get people asking for your recipe.

And of course, we say "yes" and share that recipe – practicing our 'Showing & Sharing Your Work' skill. Just think of TV Chefs, the more they share, the more good things come their way.

Bon Appetit! ... Break a leg.

MEETINGS

I don't think there is anything more varied than the experiences we have with meetings. They come in all shapes and sizes. Formal; informal; adhoc; scheduled; 1:1, team meeting, committee meeting; board meeting… everything in between. And they all leave a different taste in our mouths

If we compare this to the humble potato (of which there are over 4000 varieties, just like meetings) we soon find out using the wrong potato can change the taste, texture, and enjoyment of the dish. Specific potatoes are required for the type of dish we want to serve. The Desiree and Nicola potato are best used for mashing and making gnocchi, as it doesn't discolour after cooking, while the Kipler is best used in salads and baking. Importantly, the Sebago is best for making chips (french fries). If we extend this metaphor to meetings, depending on what outcome you want from the meeting, your choice of meeting format, and how you host it will differ. It is good to experiment with the different ingredients, and with the feedback from your meeting participants, you can tweak the recipe to get the best outcome.

I am sure you have heard us talk about "Better Together". Improving the collaboration and communications experience for your employees takes more than one product or experience. If we assume your meetings are going to take place in Microsoft Teams, here are some examples of better together pairings:

1. Microsoft Teams and SharePoint – the ability to add broad news and communications functionality with modern sites; document lists and libraries with custom metadata and workflows – allowing for a consistent process around your meeting

2. Microsoft Teams and Planner – simple task/action/or agenda management for everyone in the meeting

3. Microsoft Teams and PowerBI – Integrated data visualisation tools to empower data driven decisions within your meeting

4. Microsoft Teams and Yammer – Collaboration for beyond the meeting to get the insights and perspectives from your broader organisation
5. Microsoft Teams with Forms (with PowerAutomate) – Data gathering and activation with cross product, out of the box workflows that help capture structured, and unstructured data.

Exploring the meeting lifecycle

Irrespective of the meeting type, there are three phases of the meeting lifecycle we can explore: Pre-meeting, during meeting, and post meeting. As shown in the below image.

Meetings Flow		
Style of meeting	Formal	Informal
Typical scenarios	Committees and Communities of Practice	One on One and Stand up meetings
Before the meeting Create the calendar appointment	🟦	🟦
Create a Draft Agenda	🟦	🟦🟥🟪
Additional items provided for the meeting	🟦🟥🟩🟪	🟦🟥🟩🟪
Convert official material to PDF	📕	
Upload / Save completed agenda and additional items to Teams folder	🟪	
During the meeting Setup Teams Tabs to show additional items (as required)	🟪	🟪
Start Video Conference from invite link (if needed)	🟪	🟪
Discuss the Agenda and present additional items	🟪	🟪
Draft meeting minutes are taken	🟦	🟦
After the meeting Tasks Assigned	✓👥	✓👥
Minutes Updated	🟦	
Minutes reviewed and agreed	🟪	🟪🟦
Official Minutes distributed	📕	🟪🟦
Tasks updated	✓👥	✓👥
Tasks recorded	✓👥🟩	✓👥

Like any good meal, if you prepare well, this will give you the best chance of achieving the outcome that you want. Here is an example of how you might prepare for, deliver, and follow up your meeting:

1. Pre-meeting
   a. Creating invite
   b. Upload agenda, minutes, and additional prereading items

c. Read the materials
   d. Prepare for the meeting
   e. Set up Tabs
   f. Create OneNote Page
   g. Chat with attendees
2. During a meeting
   a. Record meeting - Video / OneNote / Minutes
   b. Co-create minutes
   c. Contribute to the meeting either verbally, visually or input into a Whiteboard
   d. Assign tasks in Planner
   e. Be present
3. Post Meeting
   a. Planner Tasks tracked and updated
   b. Create a Chat Group for 1:1 / 1:n conversation regarding the Task
   c. Co-author a document
   d. Review meeting recording or notes

The application set that you choose will depend on the many factors that go into making a good meeting experience. What's the outcome you want to achieve? Can you use the video for everyone or is the bandwidth patchy? How do you collect that instant feedback you used to get in face-to-face meetings? What rules will be in place for interactions? Do all the attendees have a level of digital literacy to use the tools that are available to them in a way that will enhance and not hinder the meeting?

Where do meetings live?

I imagine that sounds like a strange question, but it is an important one. In a traditional workplace (before we embraced hybrid work) the answer was relatively straight forward. Meetings occurred in meeting rooms. It could be a small two-person meeting room behind reception. Or it could be in a large space that can hold hundreds of people. Based on the space that the meeting was being held in, we could interpret the style of purpose of the meeting. A small quiet room signalled a more intimate, interactive conversation, potentially about a specific issue or an important issue. A meeting room with 12 seats signalled a team meeting where someone will likely chair the meeting and invite people to participate throughout the conversation. An event space signalled that this was going to be a one-way conversation, where we watch one or more speakers share their insights, knowledge, or commentary.

In a hybrid world, where every meeting is a video call, we lose those signals. Every meeting is the same pre meeting screen, where we adjust our video or audio settings, then we hit join.

Whilst this common experience across meetings is fantastic when you build your muscle memory of where to click to join the call, it removes the ritual of leaving your desk, walking to a room, and 'experiencing' the transition from your business-as-usual work, and into a space that sets the tone for your meeting.

This gets even more complicated when we have some of our team who are in the office, and some who are working from home. Where does the meeting occur? In the meeting room on the second floor, where remote participants dial in… or in the digital world?

This is one of the fundamental questions that you need to answer for yourself when embracing hybrid work. In our context, we have decided that meetings are "remote by default". The meeting occurs in the digital world – Microsoft Teams. It doesn't matter if you are joining via your laptop, or joining via a dedicated meeting room set up, our focus for the conversation is to contribute to the virtual call, and not to just broadcast a conversation from a physical meeting space. This philosophy equals the playing field in terms of access to the meeting and contributing to the outcomes of the conversation.

Beyond the physical space, we try (as much as we can) to think of meetings not as just one-off events, but conversations in the context of a larger process, journey, or initiative within an organisation. How do we connect past discussions, ideas, concepts, and decisions, with meeting at hand, and the follow up actions? Meetings should happen in context, not as a lone event in our digital workplace. This leads us to our second decisions when it comes to hybrid work – those meetings take place in the context of our work. Practically, that means we create our meetings in a Channel within Microsoft Teams (in the context of our work) vs as an individual, one-off meeting that we send to everyone's Outlook calendars.

In the following recipes in which we describe different meeting types, you will recognise that we put this philosophy into practice. Having our meetings 'live' inside a relevant Channel in a Team allows us to maintain the context of our work around the meeting – before, during, and afterwards – and make it accessible for all meeting participants. It also signals what the type of meeting is going to be before we get there.

Let's dive into a few meeting recipes and explore the different ways we can improve the efficiency and effectiveness of our different meeting experiences.

Employee (1:1)

Think of this as your humble fries that you would enjoy at the football or watching the waves roll in at your local beach. All the necessary ingredients are in one place, and it is easy to move from one owner to another over time. You just have to know the purpose and what outcomes you want from the Microsoft Team.
Is it for:

- Building a trusting relationship?
- Staying informed and aligned?
- Providing feedback to help each other?
- Focusing on topics that normally get lost in the noise (e.g., career development)?
- A combination of the above?

Here is an example of a model we call a "Employee Experience" team. It is a space where you can (in a secure way) have an ongoing dialogue between an individual and their direct report. Blending conversations about your employment relationship, with your 1:1 meetings, and formal learning or training requirements. If we recognise that our regular 1:1 meetings are an important part of this ongoing dialogue... then this is the perfect place for our 1:1 meeting to occur.

Ingredients:
- Microsoft Teams: Private Team
- Members: 2 - Employee and Manager
- Channels: 1:1s, Career Development, Feedback
- Tabs:
    - General: Purpose statement
    - Posts: any updates or discussions that need to be made outside of the meeting/catch up
    - Files: Position Description, Contract, Performance reviews, Learning Plan
    - Planner: To manage any tasks set out during the meeting/catch up

Pre-meeting

Set up the recurring meeting in the Team channel so that your manager and yourself and can have the discussions and trust that no one else can view. Create the meeting invite in Microsoft Teams through the Teams calendar and add the Channel so all meetings are in one place, which will make for easier referencing.

During the meeting

Depending on the agreed format you may only need to use the Microsoft Team to hold the meeting, for adhoc conversations and saving Files. OneNote will be for meeting notes and Planner for tasks generated out of the meeting.

Post meeting

Summarise your discussion and post it to the conversation in the 1:1 channel. Update Planner as you complete the agreed actions from the meeting

Team

So now we move onto the loaded fries' option, still a less formal affair but with a few more ingredients and a bit more preparation. Team meetings come in a variety of flavours that are specific to the team and its purpose. It could be a regular cheese fries for your department or a spicy nachos fries for the project team.

The basics are the same it's just the toppings that are different. So, let's get cooking!

Ingredients:
- Microsoft Teams: Private Team
- Members: The members of your team or project
- Channels: Meetings, Deliverables, Budget, HR, Tips and Tricks, SandPit etc. as per agreed purpose of the Team. You may create the HR or Budget Channels as Private, but this will come down to the purpose of the Channel.

Tabs:
- Posts: Requests for updates to the agenda, publishing the final agenda, announcing the pre reading documents and files, and any updates that the team need
- Files: Set up subfolders that hold the files specific for a meeting. Makes it easier to find that reference document that was presented. Agreed naming convention might be YYYYMMDD for each meeting.
- OneNote: Shared Team, to put the meeting minutes and for the team members to put their notes in
- Planner: Why else have a meeting if not to have actions prioritised and assigned?
- Specific files associated to the meeting such as the agenda, presentation files etc.

Pre-meeting

Create the meeting invite in Microsoft Teams through the Teams calendar and add the channel so all meetings are in one place which will make for easier referencing.

Load your tabs with the latest agenda, pre-reading, or the presentations that will be discussed during the meeting e.g., Budget spreadsheets, Project reports, useful websites.

During the meeting

The formality of the meeting and the outputs required will dictate how the meeting is conducted. You probably have staff working from home, meaning the meeting will be held over video conference. Recording the meeting and then have the transcription form your meeting minutes is a great way to save time and allows the unfortunate individual who takes the notes the freedom to now participate in the meeting. Or for those on leave to catch up on the recording when they are back online. Otherwise, the minute taker could write up the notes in the shared OneNote along with the other attendees or just take their own notes in the personal OneNote.

The agenda will be opened from the tab. You could leave it as an editable document that you could update during the meeting such as a Word document or this may be a PDF to adhere to auditing processes.

Post meeting

The individual or meeting coordinator will assign staff a Planner task as needed. The individuals will then work through the task and update accordingly. Remember, anyone in the Microsoft Team can view the Planner tasks and assist if required. This also saves time in trying to understand where the tasks are up to and who is working on what as the whole Team can view the Planner board.

As for the meeting minutes, they can be reviewed and uploaded into the meeting folder and then announced in the Team conversation. Depending on the formality you may create make the document a read only or PDF document.

Committee

*A committee is a group of men who keep minutes
and waste hours*
– Milton Berle

Ingredients:
- Microsoft Teams: Private Team
- Members: The committee will usually include a chairperson, as well as the members of the committee. Assistants may also be added to the Team if they are to coordinate the meetings and assigned tasks or to take the minutes.

- Channels: General, Meetings, Deliverables, Budget, HR, Projects etc. As per agreed purpose of the Team. The general tab will have the purpose statement or terms of reference. Any announcements that the whole committee need to know will also be in the general channel.

Tabs:
- Posts: Requests for updates to the agenda, announcements of the publishing of the final minutes (PDF) and agenda (PDF), announcing the pre reading documents and files and any updates that the team need to be made aware.
- Files: Set up subfolders that hold the files specific for a meeting. Makes it easier to find that reference document that was presented. Agreed naming convention might be YYYYMMDD for each meeting. The final versions of documents (agenda and minutes) will be PDF'd and uploaded to the right folder.
- OneNote: Shared Team, to put the meeting minutes and for the team members to put their notes in. As notes are generally deemed as a record there needs to be processes around the way these are handled.
- Planner: Why else have a meeting if not to have work assigned?
- Meeting associated files such as the agenda, presentation files etc.

Pre-meeting

No doubt that the meeting is a recurring meeting set well in advance but as with most meetings create the meeting invite in Microsoft Teams through the Teams calendar and add the channel so all meetings are in one place which will make for easier referencing.

Load your tabs with the latest agenda, pre-reading or the presentations that will be discussed during the meeting e.g., budget spreadsheets, project reports, useful websites.

During the meeting

The agenda PDF will be opened from the tab so everyone can view it. Meeting minutes will be taken using OneNote or a templated Word document.

Post meeting

The individual or meeting coordinator will assign staff a Planner task as needed. The individuals will then work through the task and update accordingly. Remember anyone in the Microsoft Team can view the Planner tasks and assist if required. This also saves time in trying to understand where the tasks are up to and who is working on what as the whole Team can view the Planner board.

As for the meeting minutes, they can be updated using into a template and then reviewed by the chairperson. Once officiated the template can be uploaded into the meeting folder and announced in the Team conversation.

Just like the traditional scalloped potatoes these meetings take a little more time to prepare, as you don't want to end up with a watery potato casserole just because you went with the low-fat milk and not the heavy set cream. Once you have the right technique and ingredients then the committee meeting should be easy to manage due to their structured and repeating nature. Given that a committee represents a larger group, or the organisation and members make decisions or plans on behalf of that group or organisation, you can see the need for more rigour around the reporting and documentation. This leads to additional coordination and processes.

Board

Board meetings are far more regulated than normal team meetings and just like a true French gratin dauphinoise you do not want to deviate from the standard. All the boards we have worked with have many commonalities. Not all members have organisational accounts – no corporate email or network account. Their meetings are held regularly, but they may break into smaller committee meetings or 1:1s from time to time. Their pre-reading material could easily be a ream of paper thick so there is a lot of printing and a lot of highlighting and markups-to be made. So how are members currently getting or being advised of updates? Is there a risk for a security incident with paper or emails being sent?

It is also done mostly via email or ad-hoc conversations. As well as wasting time, this process exposes businesses to unnecessary security risks. Although the members are invited well in advance there is always the possibility that one member may not be able to attend – do you postpone or simply have a video conference?

Before you create your Microsoft Team for the Board you will need to address the issue around secure connectivity for all members. Do you provide all members with a corporate account? Do you allow Guest access to the members? How do you enforce your company security policies with these individuals that may only touch your environment for a handful of days in a year? Do they adhere to the standard ways of working with company devices or do you manage their private devices? If they sync or download the papers to their own devices, how can you protect the information and maintain the confidentiality and integrity?

There are many benefits of working within the one ecosystem such as Microsoft Teams like having the documentation and meeting files in a single secure location rather than printing the papers and posting them to the individuals. Some other benefits also include:

- Applying governance and GDPR compliance policies to meeting content
- Archiving meeting content for easy retrieval later
- Removing the need to learn many different applications just to attend a meeting
- Providing access to meetings from anywhere using any device

We encourage you to speak to your Company Secretary, Chair of the Board, or corporate governance expert before putting this recipe into practice. There are valid corporate governance reasons why an independent non-executive director may not want to have any of their meeting notes or marked up board papers accessible via your corporate system. Whilst we can create a great space for collaboration to occur, your board members may not use all the features you provide.

Ingredients:
- Microsoft Teams: Private Team
- Members: Board members, and any stakeholders who support the effective running of the board
- Channels: General, Meetings, and channels aligned to the committees of the board (for example, remuneration, risk, health and safety) The general tab of each channel will have the purpose statement

or terms of reference. Any announcements that the whole board need to know will also be in the general channel.

Tabs:
- Posts: requests for updates to the agenda, announcements of the publishing of the final minutes (PDF) and agenda (PDF), announcing the pre reading documents and files and any updates that the team need to be made aware
- Files: Set up subfolders that hold the files specific for a meeting. Makes it easier to find that reference document that was presented. Agreed folder naming convention might be YYYYMMDD for each meeting. The Final versions of documents (Agenda and minutes) will be PDF'd and uploaded to the right folder
- OneNote: Shared Team, to put the meeting minutes and for the team members to put their notes in. As notes are generally deemed as a record there needs to be processes around the way these are handled
- Planner: Why else have a meeting if not to have work assigned? From our experience the tasks are not usually given to the board members but more to their assistants or the Chair will assign themselves the tasks
- Meeting associated files such as the agenda, presentation files etc.

Pre-meeting

Meeting created in the team channel.

Members invited and added as required attendees so that they receive a calendar invite via email.

Email sent to the members with the document link attached.

Load your tabs with the latest agenda, pre-reading, or the presentations that will be discussed during the meeting eg. Budget spreadsheets, project reports, useful websites.

During the meeting

The agenda PDF will be opened from the tab so everyone can work through it. Meeting minutes will be taken by the company secretary or their delegate using OneNote or a templated Word document.

Post meeting

The meeting coordinator will assign themselves or an admin assistant the Planner task as needed. The individuals will then work through the task and update accordingly, or the updates are provided at the next session.

As for the meeting minutes, they can be updated using into a template and then reviewed by the chairperson. Once agreed, the template can be uploaded into the meeting folder and announced in the Team conversation, or a link sent through email.

Company Wide

Now we move to a different type of meeting, where the focus is on pushing out material or information and not so much the interactive and collaborative team meeting we would have with our colleagues. This type of meeting is more for large scale town hall events or webinar where presenters can broadcast their presentations and attendees ask questions through a moderated chat. This is the Pomme Puree or French Style Mashed Potato style meeting nee Event. Simple to create, some core ingredients that need to be in the right proportions or it will fail and become very oily.

Similar to the Board or Committee meeting there are key roles in a Live Event.

The organiser sets up the meeting itself by inviting the presenters and producers, ensuring the Q&A and the video recording options are selected (if required).

The producer is the executive chef in this situation and controls the production of the event. Having a sous chef is a need as you never know if the chef needs to assist elsewhere or their network drops out, so trained support is always welcome.

The presenters are the ones that everyone is focused on and who are the faces of the event. These pastry chefs are cut from of the same cloth as most chefs and can function under high pressure and at a quick pace, but they often possess a higher level of patience. These staff put the icing on the cake.

The moderators who are commis chef of this kitchen do the heavy lifting when it comes to the Q&A. They need to be skilled enough to answer the questions but knowledgeable enough to know when to get assistance or to hold back a question for later.

The attendees – your guests – have the pleasure of receiving an invite to the event and with just a couple of clicks come into the event and watch the proceedings, and if they want to ask a question then it's as easy as typing a text message.

Beyond the staff that I have already mentioned there is the IT technical support staff who need to be involved. Just like the kitchen hands they keep things running and need to be across the workings of the event. An example of when these staff are crucial is if your event was internal and as Teams Live Events is a unicast stream, meaning every viewer is getting their own video stream from the internet there is a lot of traffic within your network. IT would need to set up a video distribution solution to ease the congestion. Like a bus load of tourists arriving unexpectedly at your front door and taking over the restaurant, it's how you manage the situation that makes the difference.

Just like in any kitchen, too many chefs will spoil the broth. What you need in this situation is a cue sheet and an executive chef to pull things together. The cue sheet is typically created by the producer with the input of the rest of the team, in particular the presenters. What you will have in the sheet will be a list of all the contacts involved in the event. If something goes amiss, then you want to get to the person who can help fast. The sheet will also step out the script as to how the event will proceed. Timings against the slides used, transitions to the different presenters or time where the presenter will be on screen and not just the slide deck. All the details need to be discussed so no one is caught off guard and everyone knows their place.

Rehearsals are crucial and need to happen well before the main event. If this is your first go at running an event the testing and planning should take place a couple of weeks out from the event so you can test the assumptions and play out the script. Presenters can then hone their speech to the slides, and producers can create seamless transitions. It's also a good time to test the equipment, the presenter's surroundings, the network and prepare some questions to get the Q&A going.

Ingredients:
- Microsoft Teams: Live Event
- Roles – Producer, Presenter, Attendee, IT Support
- Personas: Organiser, Producer, Presenter, Moderator, Support
- Presentation materials

Pre-meeting
- Organiser creates the Live Event appointment with producers and presenters invited

- Organiser formats the invite for the attendees and includes the Live Event link
- Organiser may also create the Microsoft Form to capture attendee details
- Producer organises the creation of the cue sheet
- Presenter creates their presentation
- Production team rehearses the cue sheet
- Publicise the event
- Join the Live Event early to test

During the meeting
- Run as per the cue sheet
- Attendees watch and participate through the Q&A
- Moderators answer the Q&A

Post-Meeting
- Producer holds a debrief with the production team
- Capture Q&A and follow up
- Publish the recording for attendees who were not able to attend
- Review the attendee list to see how long most people stayed
- Thank the audience for their participation

EMPLOYEE INDUCTION

"Onboarding is an art. Each new employee brings with them a potential to achieve and succeed. To lose the energy of a new hire through poor onboarding is an opportunity lost"
– Sarah Wetzel

They say that first impressions last. Think back to the last time you visited a restaurant for the first time. You sit down, take in the décor and the ambiance. Then it hits you… the amazing fragrance of the dish that the wait staff just walked past your table. It smells incredible. At that stage you almost know for sure you are doing to have a great meal.

The same first impressions apply when we start work with a new organisation. The experience we have in the few weeks prior to joining the organisation. The experience we have on our first day. The experience we have over the weeks and months that follow as we find our feet – they all create a first impression for new starters.

Whilst it might seem like common sense, when employees perceive that they have had a great onboarding or induction experience, they are more likely to be more successful in their role, stay longer with the organisation, and work in a more safe, less risky way (see Ingersoll & Strong 2011 if you want to dive deeper into one example of many in the literature).

What can we do design an onboarding experience (powered by some of the tools we have at our fingertips) that creates a great first impression?

Map out your onboarding process

There are a few lenses you can view the first three months of your new starters' journey.

First is the individual view, ensuring that all the appropriate paperwork is complete, all compulsory reading or training is attended to, and they have the tools and support they need to effectively contribute.

Second is the team view – how do we ensure that we set the new starter up for success where their strengths can complement the team, and the strengths of the team can complement the new starter. Where our processes or established practices are shared and embraced. Finally, there is an organisation-wide view – the new starter and their identity as an employee of your company. As they are joining a broad community in which they will do their work, how can we ensure they are connected to the greater purpose, values, and connections that exist within that community?

A simple employee induction recipe

In this example, we bring all of your new starters together into an Onboarding Team. People who join the organisation are added to this team on their first day. It has channels that relate to their employment journey over the next few months, with relevant resources in each channel attached as tabs. In parallel, we have a PowerAuotmate flow that is drip feeding email prompts to new starters over their first three months. Once their three months is up, invite people to leave the team, or hang around and answer questions of the new starters who are joining the organisation

Ingredients:
- Microsoft Teams
- PowerAutomate
- Microsoft Forms

Method:
- Create a Team called "Welcome to <your organisation name.>
- Create channels that align to your new starter's employment journey. For example
  - Your first week

- o Vision and Values
- o Mandatory Training
- o Health and Safety
- o Your questions answered
- In each channel, add relevant or important resources as Tabs. These could be pre-recorded videos, PDFs, or web pages
- Schedule your onboarding calls or induction training as recurring meetings in the appropriate channel. That way your speakers know when they will occur throughout the year, and your new starters will see the next opportunity they have to attend the training or workshop
- Using PowerAutomate, create a flow that is triggered when someone joins this Team. Using the email and delay actions, set up a flow that sends a welcome email on day one, a "check in" email on day 7, and a "if you need help with your mandatory training we are here to help" email on day 21"
- Encourage your leaders to join the Team as well to create a strong connection with new starters, and to answer any questions they may have
- Add a Microsoft Form to the "your first week" channel and encourage new starters to fill it in at the end of the first week. Add questions to the form that provide insight to the employee orientation experience and allow your new starters to provide specific feedback on their first few days

- Remember to follow up any feedback with the new starters so they know that their feedback has been heard and potentially actioned.

TRAINING WORKSHOPS

*"The goal of education is
understanding the goal of training is
performance"* – Frank Bell

Remember before COVID when we attended training in person?

Depending on where you are located around the world, it might be years since you last had the opportunity to participate in a face-to-face training workshop. Memories of sitting around tables, refilling you water, snacking on mints, and (sometimes) trying to read poorly designed PowerPoint slides as a facilitator spends a few minutes too long on an anecdote.

To be fair, there are many training facilitators who do an amazing job of creating an engaging (and entertaining) educational experience. Most built up their proficiency and effectiveness as trainers in the physical world, where you can rely on instant feedback from an audience, can seek out non-verbal signals to adjust pace. In the classroom, great facilitators can effectively manage an audience, break them into parallel discussions, engage in multiple conversations, and ultimately lead a group back towards shared understanding of a key lesson.

Speakers, trainers, and educators who are all masters in the physical world, have had to adjust to effectively deliver workshops in the digital world. Many have simply replicated the 'live' workshop experience. Audio or video of the facilitator, slides shared to the audience. The lack of feedback has reduced the efficacy of facilitators, and the miniature video feed of the facilitator off to the side of the full screen slides has reduced engagement from participants.

For many, training or workplace learning has gone backwards during the pandemic, not forwards.

There have been some great strides forward by many to reimagine what a training workshop or lecture might look like in a distributed, digital world. Whilst we don't have enough pages in this book to go into the detail of the research and science behind the decisions, one of the key lessons learned is that we can't just rely on 'synchronous' or live interactions to achieve a great learning outcome. We can't take a 'one day workshop' from the physical world and turn it into a 'one day workshop' in the digital world. We need to reimagine what training looks like (in the context of our organisation and the subject matter at hand), and create an experience that balances achieving learning outcomes, with the attention and engagement expectations of our workforce, who are grabbling with the impact of the transition to hybrid work.

What does a digital learning experience look like?

First, don't focus on the digital bit first. Instead, focus on the learning part. If you have a learning or instructional designer, or learning and development specialist in your organisation, they will be a great partner to work with in developing your learning experience.

They are specialists in Andragogy, defined by Malcolm Knowles as "the art and science of helping adults learn" – the methods and principles used in adult education. If you don't have the benefit of learning experts on hand, Collins (2004) summarised key adult learning principles, as well as questions you can ask yourself when exploring this topic. As you read through this list, think about how you could apply Teams or other parts of Microsoft 365 to answer these questions:

- **Learning is enhanced when it is immediately applicable to real-life contexts**
  - o What are some ways you can make training relevant to the learners' practices?
- **Learning is enhanced when adults have control or influence over the educational experience**

- o What are some of the ways you can give participants control over their learning?
- **Learning depends on past and current experiences**
  - o What are some of the ways you can use the learners' experiences as a resource for learning?
- **Learning depends on active involvement of the learner**
  - o What are some of the ways you can keep learners stimulated and involved?
- **Learning depends on the climate of respect and comfort**
  - o What are some of the ways you can encourage learners to be more self-directed and to continue learning on the job?
- **Learning is enhanced when learners achieve self-direction**
  - o What are some of the ways you can encourage learners to be more self-directed and to continue learning on the job?
- **Learning is enhanced when connections are created**
  - o How can you create connections among participants and the workplace?
- **Learning is enhanced when learners are successful**
  - o What are some of the ways you can help ensure that learners are successful?
- **Learning is facilitated when learners receive feedback**

o What are some of the ways you can reinforce learners and facilitate self, peer, or instructor feedback?

Putting it into action

For each of these questions, there are numerous ways we could apply the ingredients we have at our fingertips to create an improved learning experience. Let's explore! First, to enable us to put into practice many of these principles, we need to create a Team in Microsoft Teams to tie it all together. If you read our last book, you will be familiar with the 10P framework of Microsoft Teams Design – you can use that framework to design the Team specifically to the learning experience you are creating. For now, let's just assume that our Team will have a few channels:

- General – for announcements to the cohort that are engaged in the learning experience. This content can include context setting for the training – how it aligns with organisational values, issues, or other processes that are relevant to the learner
- Workshops – the channel where our synchronous workshops will be scheduled, and the recordings, transcripts, and conversations during those workshops are easily accessible for learners

- Ask me Anything – a channel where learners can ask questions about putting the learning content into practice (with answers from instructors or the learning cohort)
- Success Stories – a channel for learners to share how they have applied the learning, and the impact of that learning on their work
- Feedback – a channel to capture feedback (positive and constructive) to improve the experience over time.

You might amend that channel design depending on your content (for example, maybe additional channels to focus conversation about certain topics etc) but the above is a good start.

For each of those channels, what additional content or Tabs would make a meaningful impact on the learner's self-directed experience? There are some simple things we can do:

- Add the course of workshop outline as a PDF to the General channel
- Record a welcome video, or introductory video outlining an overview of the topic – post it to the conversation (maybe pin the conversation as well so it is at the top of the feed), then add the video as a tab for easy access by participants later
- Collate several resources relevant to the subject matter that you will talk about in the workshops,

and add them to the Workshops channel as a Word Document, or OneNote page

- Set up a shared OneNote notebook with group questions or exercises which participants could fill in during the training workshops (and add as a tab in the Workshops channel)
- Create a form to baseline understanding of the topic (add as a tab in the general channel), then use that form again at the end of your training to understand the improvement in topic understanding or application.
- Create a SharePoint Communication site, or topic page using SharePoint syntax to curate content relevant to the topic (and add as a tab so it is easily accessible).

What other examples can you think of that would be relevant? You could use Microsoft Lists or Planner to structure tasks or activities you want your learners to complete. You could encourage problem based, self-directed learning by posing questions to the group in one of the channels or using the breakout room feature inside your meeting to assign your cohort to different conversation rooms. Whatever you do, don't just go back to three hours of death by PowerPoint. This is a great opportunity to reimagine your old workshops or content, apply adult learning principles, and create a great outcome both for your learners, and your organisation.

INTERNAL COMMUNICATIONS

"Employees are drowning in information but thirsting for clarity and purpose"
– Paul Barton

Being an internal communicator is tough. They say, "communication is everyone's job", but most people don't do a great job of delivering a message, and many don't do a great job of receiving a message either.

In a previous life I had two phases of my career where I had accountability for internal communication activities. Both were in the early 2000s, where we had an explosion of digital communication channels start to emerge. The future looked bright... we might have been able to move away from the weekly staff newsletter, and towards more engaging or meaningful ways to communicate. I was wrong.

We were ten years too early. Instead, my days were filled with trying to fill the email newsletter with stories. Or proof reading or ghost-writing emails for executives afraid of saying the wrong thing.

Despite our best efforts to encourage our workforce to bring their own stories to the table, the wave of user generated content we are accustomed to today, was still in its infancy.

Today, two things have changed. First, the tools we have at our fingertips are orders of magnitude better than what was available only 20 years ago. For example, I remember paying $50,000 to hire a team to do live stream a 90-minute all-hands event across the company. Now we can do the same thing (at a better quality) by pointing an 'off-the-shelf web cam', or a mobile phone at a presenter, and with a few clicks have their presentation broadcast around the world.

We can now create, and nurture digital communicates within our organisations. We can enable self-serve consumption of content. We can 'still' create an employee newsletter, but instead of writing the story, we can simply amplify the stories of our people through curation.

Second, internal communication has changed. It is less about 'controlling' the message, and more about empowering people across the organisation to communicate in an effective way. This is important, for as the pace of change increases in our increasingly digital world, so does the need of people leading that change to be effective communicators to bring others on the journey.

There are lots of possibilities when it comes to internal communication, so whether you are professional internal communications manager, or manager or leading wanting to influence others, let's see how you can improve the way your organisation (or your department) engages in the conversation.

There are many models we could use to explore this topic (for example, Shannon & Weaver's (1949) communication process, or Daft & Lengel's Media Richness Hierarchy), however if we assume that we are communicating to guide our team or organisation through change, let's use Bill Quirke's (2008) communication escalator.

Quirke's model describes how the communication channels and tactics evolve as the degree of change, and the degree of involvement in the change increase for an individual. The five 'steps' of the escalator are:

- Awareness – we just need to be aware that something is/has changed
- Understanding – we need to understand why the change was important
- Support – we need to believe that the change is something we can support
- Involvement – we need to be involved in the change and our input is required
- Commitment – success relies on us being part of the change.

Let's explore each step of the escalator in more detail, with an emphasis on how we can use aspects of Office 365 to communicate.

Awareness

In this first step most of the communication activity we are engaging with will be one way – a broadcast – so our audience understand the essential information about the change, and how it affects them and their role.

In most organisations today, this will be achieved through an email to impacted employees. The challenge with email is that it is already an incredibly saturated communication channel, and because of the wide variety of ways that messages are delivered via email, difficult to comprehend quickly as well.

There are two things we can do in Outlook to try to overcome these challenges.

Frist, consider creating a consistent template you can use to structure your awareness communication. For example, if you are in the IT team and you want to communicate awareness of technical changes that happen semi-regularly, having a consistent format to the message could help reduce overwhelm. If your communications strategy still relies on all staff email, to create your email template, simply structure your communication (and any visual elements you might use to draw attention to it – like a coloured heading) in a new Outlook message. Then click file->Save As, and save the message as a template. You can then use the template in the future by creating a new email, then clicking the "view templates" button in the menu.

Second, consider using a consistent time you deliver the message. As your audience become used to the time that the message is delivered, they will come to expect it. Use the "Delay Delivery" feature in Outlook to set a time later in the day, next week, or anytime in the future. Once you click send, the email will not be delivered until the date and time you selected.

For organisations that rely less on email, and more on tools like Microsoft Teams, an announcement in an appropriate Microsoft Teams channel is a great way to raise awareness. Keep it short, to the point, and with a focus on the impact that the change will have on the receiver. Similar to an email template, you can use the background colour or graphic of an announcement in Microsoft Teams to provide a consistent visual queue associated with the type of announcement you are making.

Either way you make your announcement, consider how you could use a short video to support the communication. Not a full presentation, just a simple 60-90 second overview of the announcement of the change, how it might impact the workforce, and where to go for more information.

You can capture a short video using Microsoft Teams – click "Meet Now", join the meeting yourself, turn on your webcam and hit "record this meeting". Alternatively, you could simply pull out your mobile phone, record your message, then upload the video to OneDrive or SharePoint so your peers can view the content.

Understanding

At this step, we get into a little more detail. This isn't just about being aware of what is happening, we want our audience to understand why. This involves not only delivering more important or relevant information, but also providing the opportunity for people to ask questions and seek clarification. Traditionally, we have done this as a roadshow, or set up a kiosk in a high traffic area in an office. We may have presented at team meetings or set up a forum where we could physically or digitally connect to ask questions.

Whilst traditionally this step of the communication escalator would involve tactics like roadshows, videos, conferences, or stakeholder forums... In a hybrid work world where we are already overwhelmed with meetings, it could be as simple as joining a scheduled team meeting that already occurs in a Team and spending five or ten minutes of the agenda contextualising the change for that audience, and allowing the opportunity to ask specific questions. If there are overview materials of briefing papers that the group can consider, share those with the team leader or manager of that team so they can share them ahead of the presentation – if they are shared in one of their channels in Microsoft Teams, the group could review and consider the questions they wish to ask together prior to the meeting.

One way to capture how well the content was understood (and broad sentiment about the change) is to set up a Microsoft Form with a few relevant questions. You can share this as a link as part of your presentation – the easiest way is to present using PowerPoint Live in a Microsoft Teams meeting – your clickable links in the presentation are clickable by the audience as well. Alternatively, in forms you can create a QR code specific to that form. Copy the QR code into your slide pack, and your audience can use their phone to respond in real time.

Support

Traditionally in this step of the Communication Escalator you might run seminars or training courses to equip stakeholders with the knowledge they need to be successful. In a hybrid world, consider running a well-planned briefing call using Microsoft Teams with those impacted by, or who can influence the change. In structuring your briefing call, try to structure it in a way that there are 15–20-minute segments of content (with a clear transition moment at the end of each segment) to maintain or regain attention during the call.

Involvement

When we rely on our audience to be involved in the change we are communicating about – for example, there are specific activities or tasks we need them to do to make the change successful, the involvement step is vital. For example, you might be running a pilot program of an initiative that is about to roll out. Invite your key stakeholders or champions into a private or shared channel in your Team and encourage enable them to provide honest and candid feedback. Allowing them to have a voice will give them a sense of ownership in the outcome.

Commitment

Finally, we want to empower our stakeholders to champion this change or initiative with others. To do so you can keep them informed with regular updates via a SharePoint Communication site, or a Teams Channel. In that Teams Channel you can also encourage your key stakeholders to engage in additional problem solving around the initiative to keep them involved in the outcome. Or create a space where they can provide candid and explicit feedback over time. A great way to do so is to set up a Microsoft Form to capture that feedback in a structured way.

CUSTOMER SERVICE

"Customer service is the new marketing, it's what differentiates one business from another"
– Jay Baer

Our expectations as consumers have evolved over time. Whilst we can still experience great customer service from an individual (say at a store, on a service desk, or online), today customer service really is a team sport.

Our idea of 'great customer service' is still grounded in the impact of individuals, however we now expect the organisations, institutions, or departments we interact with to have a more complete picture. We expect them to understand our issue, in the context of our relationship with the organisation. We expect that irrespective of who we talk to, that we have been heard, and don't need to repeat ourselves. We expect that whether I contact you by phone, email, or social media, or a combination of the above, even if they are different teams, that the outcome should be the same. We expect that if you don't know the answer, that you know the person who does.

Whether you are working in a call centre taking calls from the public, at an internal enquiry desk on a campus, or managing a support queue, you will be acutely aware of this increased expectation.

In many organisations, this challenge is resolved using specialist customer service software. It could be a ticketing or service management system, a customer relationship management tool, or knowledge base. These tools capture and present information in a relatively structured way – great for predictability, repeatability, and management statistics. Depending on which tool you use though, it can be difficult to understand the nuance of a situation, discover who is an expert about a particular challenge, or provide positive experience that is truly memorable. One that increases customer loyalty, whilst also increases the confidence of the customer to use self-service support channels in the future.

When it comes to customer service, the tool you use to manage the case or track the ticket is only part of the equation. How you connect people, and specifically their experience and expertise to a case is equally, if not more important. So how can we use the tools at our fingertips to connect the dots between your customers, your processes, your policies, and the people who can make a real difference?

Creating a customer service/support back channel

This recipe doesn't need to be too complicated. In its simplest form, a group chat with your customer support representatives might be enough to create a 'stream of consciousness' of your team. A space where they can support each other in real time as issues or challenges occur. To create a group chat, just start a 1:1 chat with one of the team, then add participants to it. You can rename the chat to "Support back channel" or a name that is meaningful to your team.

Alternatively, a more structured Microsoft Team based approach where you have channels for support topics may be better. This particularly is powerful if you use a third-party support or customer service tool, where you could 'email' a ticket to a channel using the "email a channel" functionality in Teams. Alternatively, if you use a service desk tool that is supported by a Microsoft Teams connector, you can push a ticket to the Channel, and start a conversation with your peers, all in the context of the customer case.

To level things up, if you start using Microsoft Forms to capture customer feedback or sentiment, you can use PowerAutomate to automatically classify or redirect feedback to senior customer service representatives, or post into specific channels that will allow your retention team to proactively work on the case. To explore how you could do this, simply look at a few of the hundreds of templated PowerAutomate flows that Microsoft have made available. Those that use Microsoft Forms as a trigger. There are several which you could use 'straight out of the box' to achieve this outcome.

MARKETING

Good marketing makes the company look smart. Great marketing makes the customer feel smart"
— Joe Chernov

Product, Price, Place, Promotion. The marketing mix popularised by Neil Borden in the 1950s and refined as 'The 4 Ps of Marketing' by E. Jerome McCarthy. Each of which still play a fundamental role in how we bring products and services to market today. You need to have a great product. It needs to be priced in a way that your customers will see value. You need to distribute it so that your potential customers can get their hands on it (place). Finally, you need to promote your product or service so potential customers are aware it exists and are able to purchase.

For professionally trained marketers (myself included) we know that the 4P's in the marketing mix are critical to achieving product/market fit, and ultimately profitability (at a product, service, or organisation wide level). There are now additional Ps like 'Process' (to account for marketing automation), and 'People' (to account for the role that customer service plays in customer loyalty) that further extend the model in a meaningful way.

However, for many outside the marketing profession, today the marketing mix is reduced down to the final P – promotion. How can we use Pay Per Click advertising, Content, Collabs, Influencers, Social, Activations, NFTs, anything to get attention on our brand and our products or services?

For the purposes of this chapter (as much as it grates me to do it) we will reduce our focus down to promotion as well. And specifically look at how we can use Office 365 for content marketing. This is for two reasons. First, it will probably add another 90 pages to this book if we dive deep into marketing theory/strategy. Second, a lot of the types of work we need to do to create great products, get pricing right, and coordinate distribution systems is indirectly covered in other recipes we cover in this part of the book (like meetings, project collaboration etc). Framing this chapter around content marketing makes it easier to cover some of the novel use cases that apply to marketing, without spending hours on the topic.

So, lets focus on content marketing. Full disclosure: this book is part of our content marketing strategy. We know that if we can help our potential customers improve their confidence and capability in a low-risk way – downloading an eBook onto their eReader – more people are likely to know who we are, what value we deliver, and think of us next time a requirement comes up. We don't sell ourselves; we help others achieve what's next. It is a powerful strategy that great content focused markets use. Not just "top 10 lists" or "the three (really obvious) things you need to know about x" to game search engine rankings – we are talking about meaningful value that opens doors.

Whilst you don't need to self-publish a book (by the way, we wrote this and our last self-published book using a combination of OneNote, Teams, Planner, SharePoint, and Word), there are lots of ways you can educate your audience using Office 365.

Ironically there are thousands of different "5 step" models to guide your marketing efforts. Each with a different focus or nuance depending on whether you are interested in B2B marketing, or B2C. There isn't one 'grand unifying' content marketing framework, so instead, here are a few areas that we can focus on.

- Setting our goal, and tracking it
- Research and analysis
- Preparing content
- Delivering webinars
- Repurposing content

So, what is a quick recipe that would allow us to do the above? Again, we will ground this in a Team that we can create for our content marketing efforts. Let's call it "Content Marketing Central". Within that team there are some obvious channels we could create: Research, content development, online events, and reporting.

The research channel we can use to share ideas, resources, statistics, and other data that will help us better define our target audience. In the content development channel, we can do all the heavy lifting – co-authoring using Word to draft blog posts or long form content, or PowerPoint to prepare pitch decks. Planning for these content pieces can be coordinated using Microsoft Planner, or lists added as tabs to the channel. If you love your Excel based content calendar, simply add it as a tab to this channel so all stakeholders can see when content is due to be published.

In the Online Events channel, focus the conversation on the logistics around facilitating your webinar content. Remember that you can use Microsoft Teams to facilitate your online event as well – either using the Webinar capability to run an interactive event with a smaller group, or Live Events for a broadcast one to many scenario.

Finally, when it comes to goals and tracking them, if you are like many marketers, you will have a spreadsheet where you have perfectly modelled all the data that you can capture around a campaign – Analytics from the website, social media impressions, lead data from your CRM etc. If you have all that data at your fingertips, instead of just relying on your spreadsheet (which you could add as a tab in the "Reporting" channel, take this as an opportunity to explore how you could create a report using PowerBI. Import the data sources you use (or even the spreadsheet you have been maintaining) and then see how you can visualise that information in a way that creates meaning for yourself, and your stakeholders.

KNOWLEDGE MANAGEMENT

"We know more than we can tell"
– Michael Polanyi

You might have heard members of your Executive team say, "Our people are our greatest asset," at a recent company all hands, or at the Shareholder meeting. In many industries, where people generate value – such as the public sector, education, retail, healthcare and more... you could argue this is true. When people (vs financial capital, or infrastructure) are the primary way that value is generated, you would hope that your leadership team recognise that fact!

The real value that people bring to an organisation is not just our physical labour – it is our ideas, our experience, our expertise, our wisdom, our insight, our intuition, our talent, our observations, our judgement, our mental models, our beliefs, and our values. Even our hunches are valuable! This kind of knowledge is referred to as "tacit". The knowledge that is difficult to explain. The knowledge that is challenging to document. We might have gained it from both personal and professional experience. It may have been gained from our current job, or the vast array of previous jobs or life experiences that we have been exposed to.

This tacit knowledge (sometimes called implicit knowledge) is the value that we bring to our work. The asset that our CEO is proud of.

There are other types of knowledge that we engage with in the workplace. Facts, or "know what" are a type of descriptive knowledge, an example that can be described as "explicit knowledge" – which is far easier to capture, document, codify, and share with others in written or verbal form.

Whether we are looking at tacit knowledge – the hard to describe way of doing things that we bring to our work, or explicit knowledge – the documented resources, processes, work practices, and procedures, it is important to know that both are important in helping us achieve our goals.

Which raises the question – how do we manage or curate knowledge in a way that ensures that we can capture and share the know-how of our people, enabling our team to grow in their confidence and capability, whilst improving our processes? Then how do we help our people internalise those processes to be part of their way of doing things? A model to help us navigate this problem was developed and refined by Ikujiro Nonaka and Hirotaka Takeuchi in the 1990s. The "SECI model of knowledge dimensions" helps to articulate how tacit and explicit knowledge can be converted into organisational knowledge. There are four modes described by the model:

- Socialisation (tacit to tacit)
- Externalisation (tacit to explicit)
- Combination (explicit to explicit)
- Internalisation (explicit to tacit)

Let's explore how we can use different capabilities across Office 365 to enable this knowledge transfer.

Socialisation (tacit to tacit)

Socialisation is all about connection, trust, observation, and discovery. Encouraging your team to work in an open way – documenting their work as they go – makes a huge difference. The key here is not to just focus on the outcome, but to share the process of your work as you do it. This can be achieved in either Teams or Yammer – remembering that Yammer communities of interest are open and more discoverable by default than a Team that is structured for project-based work with a small group.

If work is shared in a more open way, it is easier for people to transfer knowledge by observing that work. It also allows the opportunity for people across your organisation to identify experts who they may want to follow or observe further. Encouraging your team to update their Office 365 profile with information like their skills, interests, and noteworthy projects helps people to identity who the experts really are.

Externalisation (tacit to explicit)

Our favourite channel in a project Team (or any Team for that matter) is "Lessons Learned". Add this channel any time you create a Team, so you have a consistent place for your colleagues to share any insights or reflections they have throughout your project, or in the flow of their work.

Capturing those lessons is only the first step though. As a Team owner, you can curate those lessons learned into meaningful posts to the rest of your team – either as a summary Word document, or an article in a SharePoint Communication site. If you have a community of practice or community of interest, share your curated and refined insights with the rest of the group, so they can learn from your experience and add their flavour to the conversation.

Combination (explicit to explicit)

If we are capturing lots of lessons learned across projects or initiatives, we need to ensure that someone has accountability, or there are systems in place to ensure that we combine and synthesise that knowledge into new ideas, frameworks, or practices for our organisation. It is a big job, and many organisations don't have a knowledge manager on staff who could support this activity. However, this is a great opportunity to leverage Viva Topics to automatically generate topic pages for your organisation. Topic Pages in Viva Topics leverage insights from Office 365 to identify important information and experts relating to the subject. Those pages can then be curated by your human experts to refine that knowledge based on the context of your organisation's work. A great way to systematise the combination of knowledge when your human knowledge management resources may be light on the ground.

Internalisation (explicit to tacit)

Finally, how do we 'internalise' all that explicit knowledge, so it just becomes the way we do things? This is really a cultural challenge – something that Office 365 doesn't solve by itself. However, you can absolutely use tools across Office 365 to make it possible. Based on our experience, this requires leadership at a team, departmental, and organisation wide level to recognise the value of knowledge in your business, and then to build processes that reinforce it. In every project we need to consider lessons learned from the past. In every performance discussion, we need to consider how we integrate key organisational knowledge into the way we approach out work.

Encouraging team members to leverage those knowledge assets that have been created (like your Viva Topic Pages, or SharePoint Articles, or those Communities of Interest where you are sharing 'codified' knowledge) will help to embed that knowledge over time.

PART FOUR:
RECIPES TO INSPIRE

Now that we have learned more about our ingredients, explored some of the skills required for great teamwork, and experimented with some common recipes for teamwork across organisations, let's dive deeper into some specific, real-world examples. We don't present these case studies as recipes for you to recreate perfectly in your organisation. Instead, their intent is to inspire. Stories that you can use to explore how different teams in different industries might solve specific problems using Office 365. Even though a recipe might not be aligned to your industry, the problem they are solving might be. These stories will spark ideas in your mind as to how you could best apply aspects of these solutions in your team or department.

We have purposely shared these stories with a bit more context, so you can see not only the recipe, but our thought process in developing the recipe itself.

We have a challenge for you as you read these recipes. What tweaks would you make? Or what ingredients would you add? Think about how you would augment these stories with tools like PowerAutomate or Microsoft Forms. What impact would having visibility to insights from Microsoft Viva would have in designing how teamwork would occur? Would you approach it differently if you had a thriving Yammer community, access to dedicated Teams Meeting rooms, or curated topic pages that connected you to the right experts in your business? Every organisation is going to have a slightly different technology landscape, and a slightly different context... so let's see how we can design a meal that works for your specific tastes. Let's dig in!

A COMMUNITY OF PRACTICE FOR MEDICAL SALES REPRESENTATIVES

Life as a sales representative in the field it can be an isolating experience. They look to be connected to HQ for support and confidence in making decisions, so they are not alone. The role of a team lead is to ensure their 'reps' have what they need to execute on what their day brings.

But having the right information at the right time isn't easy when the sales reps don't have a central place to access content and conversations and are often at the mercy of waiting for the gatekeepers (team leads) to deliver them their knowledge needs. They are often looking for information in scattered places (mostly with no luck) and chasing and waiting on what they need based on who they know. This can be frustrating when they have a full calendar day and want to provide the best customer experience possible.

In addition to this, there's a sense of urgency that is inherent in their role. When they look at their calendar and prep to visit their next customer, they can't afford this prep time to blow out their schedule. When they are in the presence of a customer, they need to be as knowledgeable as possible to answer questions or to be able to source answers in a good time frame. So, it's no surprise their main frustration is "waiting".

What do people say when they are sick of waiting? I'll do it myself. Only this wasn't that easy to do

Preparation

One of the goals of our engagement with this customer was – how do we reduce this "waiting" time?

This was an oblique path to take but doing so would have impact on things that matter. It would contribute to better customer experiences, reduce their email overwhelm and information retrieval frustrations, and it would improve their engagement and growth of learning. So how would it do this?

Being more operationally efficient in sourcing answers, means not wasting their customers time, or looking not very resourceful or knowledgeable. We could call this a reputational risk or better customer experience.

A more elegant tool than email to act as a knowledge base and decision support system would

288

reduce their frustration and increase their confidence. Let's call this improving their autonomy to get things done.

And lastly, this same technology system can build and nurture a peer community that aggregates this once scattered knowledge, providing opportunity to level-up the mastery of their game and a sense of belonginess. In a nutshell a more engaging experience and building personal brand.

Of course, the technology is there to power it all, but first is recognising the problem, purpose and behaviours required for a successful solution.

The customer relationship managers (or CRMs) at a national level needed to ensure their service met their referrer needs by providing staff effectiveness via a 'brain's trust' i.e. to be connected to their main office and to all their sales reps

The requirements were to:

- be included in the ins and outs of what's new
- self-serve the retrieval of information
- access knowledge and learn from people like me

Guarantee - this meal will not cause the following side effects!

- It is frustrating waiting for answers when you have asked a question of someone in the team. You end up with five balls in the air and you're not sure which one will drop first so you are monitoring your diary to make sure that you can fulfill the need for the customer

- We don't have a good way to leverage each other's knowledge, nor look back at what was done before... which is even more amplified for new starters. For example, I'd like to ask peers – How do your customers respond to the material that you are using for vascular ultrasound? How do you use your material when targeting gastroenterologists?

- Having to look around for a document from three months ago, not remembering whether it was an email attachment, in a share drive, etc… and then if found not knowing if it's the current version. When on our visits we need to be quicker and more confident in our information foraging

- As a team lead, I feel I'm always being asked to repeat the same information. I want to reduce the amount of email trails and confusion when someone misses the email or doesn't get cc'd in

- Being field based, we are in and out of clinics and are not able to answer our phones or respond to messages. Sometimes, it is the next day before I can respond to the message. It would be more efficient to have a page where you can look and search to see what was available and what the responses were.

Ingredients

- Microsoft Teams
- Channels
- Tabs
- Files
- Mobile App

Method

The key change was to move to a self-service peer model, where each CRM could access the content and people required to support their work. As we heard above, they were not connected enough to effectively be in the loop and source content, which meant some of them missed out on conversations or had different information/understanding about the same topic.

The Team in Microsoft Teams would be *the* place for CRMs to connect and support each other about know-how e.g. sharing experiences, stories, asking questions, getting advice, leveraging each other's local offerings, not having to re-invent the wheel – and ultimately help each other make sense of things and increase the effectiveness of their daily workflows.

In essence it would formalise the multiple existing pockets of personal networks where the reps reach out to each other for advice, and act as a visible source of truth way for leadership to update sales reps with the latest information and happenings.

This Community of Practice would cover nationally relevant topics (eg. Covid-19) as well as topics for each modality (eg. MRI) – this was especially important for quick access and findability to information, and for triaging priority and what matters most to an individual.

CRM National Connection

- Ultrasound
- MRI
- CT
- Mammography
- PET
- Medicare benefits
- Telehealth (e-referrals)
- Sales

- Salesforce updates
- Covid-19
- Competitor information
- Articles of interest

One of our rules of thumb is for a Team to have under seven channels otherwise there are too many focus areas to spread your effort and get things done. But there was an exception in this case.

Yes, there are a lot of channels, but they are serving only two priorities. Those being updates, questions and accessing information on – national topics and on modality topics. We found all the channels in this Team are contributing to achieving the specific purpose and problem being solved.

After co-designing their Team to align it to improve their daily outcomes, it was then onto onboarding members and coaching them for success. A big part of this was the proverbial pinning the Rules of Engagement on the board (for this we used a Wiki tab). The main rules were:

1. We encourage all members to contribute in a positive way. To be supportive, share ideas, experiences and answers that allows others to develop their skills and be as productive as possible

2. Participation regardless of CRM experience is encouraged. Contribution and engagement will

ensure this Team is a highly useful and valued resource

3. This Team is National – so not for 'Local/State CRM activity/content i.e. clinic openings, daily activities, local competitor activity. There will be Local/State Teams set up for these conversations and activity.

The 'answer or solution' is not always going to be found in the new Team we co-designed, however the hope was that from interacting with this Team a CRM would be pointed in the right direction to find the content, advice or resources they required.

And could the Teams mobile app be any more aptly suited to a use case. Get what you want wherever you are on your tablet or phone. We don't even have to mention how essential this is to a sales field rep, it's almost a given these days.

Secret Sauce – Channels and much more

The secret sauce in our recipe was simple and obvious. Isn't that the case with all great things!

Time is of the essence

It was essential their work was to be organised by topic, as time is not a luxury in the field to sift through your last month of emails trying to locate a particular conversation about MRI's - *'oh, there it is in the MRI channel'* is quite a comforting feeling.

Speed and confidence

But even more rudimentary than channels that supported time poor sales reps in the field, is the simple but effective design of threaded conversations. Now there's only one threaded conversation about something, rather than weaving together a conversation from seven different emails, minus the emails about the same conversation you don't even know exists. This not only helped with saving time but gave more confidence in knowing this was all there was to see.

All the things, with none of the pings

Given the volume of conversations and knowledge across the Sales role, it's now magical that you have visibility to conversations that you aren't even in, without the expense and overwhelm of having to be pinged. That's right, access to everything without being notified every minute. Just dip in when you want later.

What you want, when you want

And when time *is* a luxury, and a sales rep would like to catch up with content – the triaging process kicks in where the individual can choose what topic they want to read first, rather than starting at the top in an email inbox. Or they could start with reading the items in their activity feed as these items are the current conversations, they are in.

Check for seasoning

To test the effectiveness of what we were building it was best to start some early testing with a sample of members by asking them to throw some typical questions at it:

"Has anyone any case studies around Vascular Ultrasound? "
• Ultrasound channel… check.

"I need some advice regarding a referrer… does anyone find this? Any suggestions on how I can handle this? "
• Telehealth (e-referrals) channel… check (with a tab to the e-referral request website)

"Is an Occult fracture listed on a referral considered a clinical indicator for Medicare benefits for a musculoskeletal ultrasound?"

- MBS (Medicare Benefits Schedule) information channel…check (with a tab to the MBS website and a files library of the latest reference sheets.)

"I have just received some additional COVID-19 WHS information from our WHS manager. Any comments/questions please reply here."
- Covid-19 channel… check (with links to the Files for the policies/procedures)

"The bookings portal has had a facelift, so for those of you who have been using this for your e-Referral call planning, you may like to note these changes below…"
- Telehealth (e-referrals) channel… check (with a tab to the e-referral request website)

So how was your meal?

For the recipe to taste right we had to hit this goal: 'I'll know this is successful when we have better connection and support for our CRMs from HQ.'

We have a daily place where we can engage to ensure we feel connected to our colleagues, an opportunity to demonstrate our know-how, and receive help and guidance from the crowd

- We have support and confidence in making decisions, so we are not alone

- Every rep feels supported and confident in making decisions in the time frame they need

- Every rep feels connected to HQ and in the loop of the latest discussions and documentation

- Quicker responses to referrers about their questions and concerns

Our focus was a shift to a self-service/peer connection model to improve their pain points in access to content and people to get their work done effectively. As this unfolded with the required new shared purpose, processes and behaviours and the technology to power it all - we were happy to know it was set up to serve their social operating human requirements of empowerment, autonomy, engagement, connecting to others, and building their repertoire of knowledge.

Kitchen Talk

Often there's a divide – where the stance is taken that Yammer is a more aptly designed tool for a Community of Practice, over Microsoft Teams. This is no surprise given the online group spaces in a Yammer network are called "Communities". Something that solidifies this further is the generally held assumption that Teams is where you do your 'bread and butter' interdependent work with people you frequently work with daily/weekly (eg. projects, teams), and Yammer is where you go to connect with the organisation-at-large to learn, discover, and engage (i.e. bridging silos). We bring back smarts from Yammer to apply to our work in Microsoft Teams – Yammer as brains trust and culture builder.

We like this contrast that work and deliverables are done in Teams, and organisation-wide conversations, communities and culture is done in Yammer – it puts us in the right headspace. Our perspective is that whilst we are in planning meetings and working on deliverables in Teams, we don't want the noise, interruptions, or distractions of what *should* be happening in Yammer.

But given all this, it's important to discover what people are trying to achieve, before jumping into a technology decision.

Indeed, Yammer's design lends well to a Community of Practice as it enables like-minded people who may work in different business units and locations to *discover* each other and come together to learn and build their knowledge.

It is worth diving deeper on what we mean by 'discovery' in this context.

Yes, you can search the Microsoft Teams directory by Team name to discover a Team you may be interested in. But this discovery attribute is pale in comparison to searching Yammer – which searches not just the names of Yammer communities but searches the content of every community in the Yammer network. Further to this you can read and post in a Yammer Community without needing to become a member of it.

But I digress – back to the point. Yammer's strength is in *visibility and discovery* of content that leads to connecting people, whereas Microsoft Teams is not quite designed with this as its primary focus.

In this case, the customer's organisation had not adopted Yammer, so Microsoft Teams was something secure and available to them to still achieve their outcomes. But more specifically – this use case was not a strict Community of Practice. Although it was voluntary and designed to help inform and connect CRM staff to content and each other to support them in doing their work – it was also business unit-like in that updates and questions about the CRM role were handled in this space. So, it's not just about learning and knowledge to grow expertise in your sales rep role, it's about a reference library and important communications you need to know to do your job. In essence, CRM was applying *community* attributes to the CRM practice.

Additionally, the attraction of Teams-as a technology choice for their use case-was in organising their numerous topic areas into channels, making use of Tabs and organising files in folders – affordances that are absent in Yammer.

So, the point of Kitchen talk is – before jumping to a technology choice, it's paramount to listen to the problems and user experience that is being addressed. Often the tool you had in mind before going into a discovery workshop with a small group of people, may end up not being the best choice for their context.

STREAMLINE ADMINISTRATIVE WORK IN THE ACADEMIC SERVICES OFFICE

When I first met with the team of an Academic Services office, we were waiting for one of their staff to arrive before we could make a start. After a few minutes of waiting the Team lead excused herself to go fetch the late comer. When she came back into the room, she began to explain to us why one of her staff would be late and to start without her. And just like that the session kicked-off with the Team leads frustration of needing to share her pain points right there and then of what caused her staff member to be late. She was not late because of a flat tyre, or because she slept in – she was late due to their teamwork processes not being visible and collaborative enough. It was not her fault; the fault was in their processes.

The processes of this team are all about servicing and managing the needs and requirements of the Academic office of a scientific discipline in their university. This includes liaising with academics, and other parties in organising and managing things like exams, timetabling, misconduct, honours programs, seminars, events, etc. They also run a front office counter to take enquiries from students and other parties that visit their building.

If we were to point out their biggest pain point it would be visibility into the progress of a task. Situational awareness is super important to this team as they are made up of a lot of part-time workers who finish off each other's tasks – if someone is not in, someone else needs to be able to fill in their shoes and pick up where they left off. They needed to reduce occurrences of, 'I didn't know about that,' 'I can't find that as she's not in today,' 'I'll have to get back to you to find out where we are at with this,' 'sorry about the delay.'

Bad weather wasn't causing delays, it was their teamwork processes. And the delay that caused the tardiness of, let's call her Sally, to our workshop that morning was the lack of visibility into Sally's daily work interactions. Sally (who is part-time and was away the previous day) was emailed the previous day by her co-worker to finish off an activity. So, Sally had to action it in the morning, which made her late to our workshop. The Team lead asked how we can prevent this, and added that if she had known about this task, she could have finished it off herself when she arrived in the early morning or even in the afternoon of the previous day (even before Sally got a chance to read the message). But she could not as she didn't know about it; it wasn't visible to her; it was only visible in the inboxes of two people.

The Team lead continued that it could get even worse. This visibility issue is amplified when someone calls in sick. For example, if Sally called in sick today, and an internal customer called about the progress of an activity, she would not know how to help the customer – 'I would have to call, chase, hunt around for the information – causing delays and negatively impacting our customer experience,' she said.

Plain and simple there was not enough situational awareness of where they were at with their tasks and operations at any given time. The part-time makeup of their team has put extra pressure on them to be more aligned and connected. Often there's confusion or too much time spent on figuring out where they are up to on a given activity. Too many daily handover meetings take place, and they take time. Too many post-it notes to inform each other of progress. Constantly chasing each other for responses and actions.

This had an impact on the quality of their service, evident by comments made by academic staff such as, 'I need to speak to Megan as she knows what is going on.' Something had to change.

Preparation

It was quite clear the Team lead was looking to change the way they work to be more visible. To enable them to 'self-serve' progress updates on their activities. It was key their staff could easily pick-up where others left off and be more informed of what others in the team were doing. This meant recording any documents and emails along with progress notes in a visible place where others could: continue working on these activities, leave updates, ask questions

They ultimately wanted academics to have confidence in all their staff – they needed to provide certainty that they know what's going on to their stakeholder groups – primarily academics, students, and visitors.

Before we start shopping for ingredients and turning the gas on let's summarise the situation. This Academic Services office relies on timely knowledge to do their job effectively:

- The part-time makeup of their team has put extra pressure on them to be more effectively aligned as a connected team
- Information comes from all angles (vital information that all don't hear, but need to know)

It is key that they can easily pick-up where others left off and be more informed of what others in the team are doing so, they can "seamlessly" serve Academic staff

Guarantee - this meal will not cause the following side effects!

- Two of their staff are part-time and work on exams – and often can cause confusion, messiness, considerable time to know "where we are up to" on a given activity

- If they are not going to be in the next day, they may need to meet to hand over just to know where they are at, what emails were sent, lots of sticky notes (additionally not all can be present at these meetings)

- If front desk staff are absent or away, they find it hard to step in their shoes and do their job for that time period, as they have no history of up to that point

- The Team lead must chase people for responses to see if they have read her email or actioned a task.

Now that we know what we need to cook, let's select what we need to buy to make this recipe

Ingredients

- 2 x Microsoft Teams
- Channels
- Meetings
- Tabs
- Files
- OneNote
- Planner

Method

It was clear that Microsoft Teams was going to be the tool of choice to manage the work they do into a centralised hub, giving visibility as well as organisation to the activities they undertake. In this way, rather than constantly chasing each other for updates, everyone's work is 'observable' as it happens, and members can self-serve the progress of all things.

As we designed a solution using the Adopt & Embrace 10Ps Teamwork Design Framework, we discovered there were a myriad of priorities, too many for one Team alone. So, we categorised these priorities across two Teams.

All staff in this Academic Services Office are members of both Microsoft Teams, but some staff spend more time in one Team than the other. In this way each Team has a clear focus, and the name of the

Team can describe the specific focus. If we were to fit all priorities into one gigantic Team, the name of the Team would be very generic and not describe well what happens in that Team.

Another important aspect that went into this decision is that it gave each 'focus' a sense of place and identity. Rather than absorbed into a generic Team, having a Team called "Communications & Mailout" gave Fiona a sense of ownership and autonomy to manage her accountabilities.

Below are the two Teams (and five channels in each Team) Note: During our engagement we soon realised a third Team would be required that revolved around the staff themselves, rather than the things they do as represented by the other two Teams. This third Team would cater to: Staff news, Staff fun, Check-in, What I'm working on today, Staff admin, etc.

For now, let's focus on the 'Teaching Team', and the 'Communications & Mailout Team

Teaching Team
- Honours & Masters
  A channel to converse and space to collaborate for the activities and tasks
  - Collection/download assessment items to send to examiners and supervisors
  - Preparation for seminars and oral examinations

- - Tabs - Planner checklist, Website link to LMS
- PhD

  To liaise with the Graduate Research unit
  - Make student appointments
  - Track and file paperwork to and from the unit
  - Tabs - Spreadsheet log, Weblinks to the Student Management System, and Graduate Research unit webpage, Document link to instructions for reporting
- Timetables

  Communicate amongst our team common student queries
  - About classes, trouble shooting a query (usually about clashes), change updates we are informed of
  - Communicate amongst our team about updates we receive and queries about class sizes, subject clashes, etc
  - Tabs - Weblinks to Class Allocation System, and Timetables, and Student Management System
- Exams

  Conversations we have had with exam staff can be shared here so our team is in the loop
  - Example - I just spoke to exams and they told us "this"
- Misconducts and Appeals

When we are communicated to about a misconduct from the Academic Conduct Advisor

- o   we use this channel to coordinate the part of the process that our Team is involved in

Communications & Mailout Team

- What's On

  A channel for the "space" so we are all aware of what's happening on a given day in our part of the building

  - o   Example – could be a morning tea, an event, visitors, etc
  - o   Tabs – Website link to Resource Booker, Link to calendars (foyer / equipment), weblink to resource booker

- Seminars

  A channel for any of our team to communicate with each other on any updates, questions, or discussion about seminars

  - o   We host a seminar series and advertise other seminars, we circulate notices, invitations to meet with speakers, and abstracts to a mailing list.
  - o   A weekly calendar is sent out at the beginning of the week and a reminder on the day of seminar

- Events

  Multiple events needing short bursts of communication / organisation

- Example – Open Day, Honours Expo, end of semester BBQ, Christmas party
- Tab – SharePoint link to events folder

- Travel & Expenses
  Managing expenses and purchases
  - Purchasing, CabCharges, reimbursements
  - Conversations with other staff can be shared here so our team is in the loop (eg. I just spoke to purchasing and they told us they would pay for the online shopping order today)
  - Exit protocol (eg. return of keys)
  - Tabs – Weblinks to expense management system, and help resources

- Committees & Meetings
  Coordinating meetings
  - Communicate when the next committee meeting is coming up including setting up and sending meeting requests, whether the chair has been contacted for agenda items, agenda circulated, and whether the academic services team member will be taking minutes/notes or arranged for someone to step in
  - Meeting notes/minutes drafted and finalised

- Tabs - Spreadsheet of committee meeting schedules and members, and SharePoint link to committees folder

It is worth mentioning here the subtle affordances that tabs and Planner bring that really make this new way of working happen:

Tabs to keep frame of focus

This team access a myriad of resources and systems, which means they have lots of things open on their computer, having to constantly switch between them. Now it's all accessible in the context of where they need it using the Tabs functionality – eg. they are in the Timetables channel knee-deep in a conversation with their colleague trouble shooting a query about a clash in the timetables. Right there, one click away they have access to the class allocation system, opening right where they are within the channel, keeping them in their frame of focus.

Planner to make sure things don't slip through the cracks

For more formal tasks the academic services office team are making use of Planner to help them visually track the tasks they have delegated across the team. And OneNote provides a centralised way to capture organic and unstructured meeting notes.

Previously their work was not documented in a task-centric way, but rather using email and post-it notes to both execute the task and to give updates on the progress and what's left to do. Hunting for these emails was a time waster and didn't provide the required assurances that everything that needed doing was accounted for. Similarly, people took their own meeting notes, and emailed them around. Not having a source of truth and quick to access storage place ran the risk of staff missing out on important information or things falling through the cracks and not making it to a task list

Secret Sauce – Send an email to a channel

A must-have for this Team was the ability to forward an email to a channel. This was a big win. It provided maximum gain, for very little behaviour change. What may look like an ordinary functionality to one Team is a game changer for another – it's all about the context and the use case.

The team were constantly receiving emails from stakeholders – and a new behaviour was to now forward them into the appropriate channel.

Example – Student misconducts

They receive an email and attachment from an academic about a student misconduct. This is forwarded into the channel where it's now stored and ongoing internal conversation about this case happens so the progress and content are visible and accessible to all team members. A typical post may be *"@team this student has been sent an email with the PDF attached. I'll let you know here when they reply to the email"*

Example – Exam papers

They receive an email and attachment of an exam paper from a coordinator and forward it into the channel, and then review the files with internal discussions. Typical posts may be *"@team I have reviewed the file, and emailed the coordinator to come in for physical checking"*, or *"@megan I had a hiccup with page numbering, but all sorted now"*

These workflows above involve numerous parties i.e. Academics, Students, Academic Services Office - but it's important to note that we are just handling the part of the process that involves the Academic Services team to improve the way *they* coordinate, communicate and collaborate with each other in these workflows.

Check for seasoning

Let's have a quick taste to see if our cooking is on the right path.

What's the latest conversation about who is paying for the food?

Simply go to the Travel & Expenses channel to see the latest post – previously this information was in someone's inbox, and you had to hunt them down to find out, hoping they were at work that day, and not having to comprise one of your principles of not contacting staff when they have a day-off

Now ask a similar question about the latest conversation on timetable changes or exam prep or next week's seminar. We can see it is now all visible where you can discover and self-serve progress – giving you more time in your day to do your work, rather than wasting time looking for stuff and holding daily meetings to get on the same page of what's going on.

This is when we knew the Team was ready to move from experiment to pilot stage.

So, how's your meal?

For the recipe to taste right we had to hit this goal:

"I'll know this is successful when we can confidently feel like we know what is going on across the Team"

- Am I across what happened yesterday? What did I miss? What do I need to know to perform today?

- We should also see a reduction in email across our team, as well as a reduction in progress meetings, and sticky note-based communication

- There will be greater confidence across the team, and less wondering if 'so and so did that thing the other day' — a diminished need to chase for progress updates.

Let's walk up to their table and ask the members how their food tastes

No more multiple file confusion
"The Exams Results checklist is something that is referred to nearly every day. Having it in a quick and accessible place with one-click edit within the Teams app, makes it a frictionless experience."

No more lack of awareness
"This is what has changed for us...If I fall off my bike on my way to work, I'm not the only one who knows about this needing to get done today."

New starter support
"As a new member of the team this type of post is priceless for me...I'm sure I would have not remembered all these steps...and if I ask for clarification in the replies, there's bound to be a member in our office that can help me (and it's good they have all the context)."

Learning from the past

"I had this same problem (page numbering difficulties on exam files) last semester, but I can't remember how I fixed it. I don't know where to start searching, I can't remember where we had that conversation. Now past conversations can easily be found by browsing the past exam files and reading the conversations (or we can do a search in Teams). Given every conversation in Teams has a link - I'm thinking about creating a link list of tips and making it available as a Tab in a channel."

Now, who's picking up the bill ;)

A CENTRAL AND CONNECTED PLACE TO ORCHESTRATE SOFTWARE RELEASES

The Release Management team coordinate quarterly releases of their software in the emerging FinTech (financial technology) industry. Although releases occur every quarter, the effort is not performed in a sequential pattern – instead, planning and work is being coordinated across all four releases in the year in parallel.

Each release relies on teamwork across various roles. A release manager, not unlike a chef, needs to orchestrate all roles involved in getting a release into production. In this case its financial software served up to the hungry guests. If you just heard 'soft serve', you'll have to wait a little longer for dessert!

Coordinating a diverse set of people that live across various teams (each with their own directors and groups cultures), and the effort of working on multiple releases in parallel – can easily become chaotic if the release manager and members involved are not organised enough and aligned with a shared purpose and agreed operations for success. So how does it work?

Whilst they are developing a release, they take requirement submissions from multiple customer projects happening at the time, as well as requests from past customer projects that didn't make previous releases. And of course, requirements that emerged from their internal experiences.

This alone, right at the start of the process, requires coordination from multiple parties to submit and consolidate requirements. It wasn't easy when requirements files lived in a myriad of shared drives and emails. This was compounded when copies of new versions begin to appear. The release manager's time became drained in clerical duties of making sure they had all the correct things they needed to proceed. This was not a good use of the release manager's time – like a chef spending too much of their time on prep and not enough in doing what they do best – cooking.

Next the release manager needs to coordinate with the development team to start discussing the tasks required to meet these requirements, as well as the effort required. Prior to working a new way this process comprised of hundreds of emails. And of course, multiple versions of the truth of what's going on within a release based on the emails you are involved in. Hence potential confusion, and a flurry of emails and meetings to constantly chase progress and realign.

And it continues with creating the technical design based on the prior requirements. Again, this involves planning and resource allocation. And exactly as above, it was a black box to the release manager, as they were not privy to the work in progress of the technical design. Constantly needing to text, call, email, meet to gain the status of things.

At the same time the release manager is coordinating with quality assurance to request and prepare a set of testers. Much the same – planning and resource allocation is devoted to developing testing tasks and scenarios. And again, we have lots of emails and meetings.

When we move into the coding stage, we have the black box scenario again where the inner workings of the dev team are unknown to the release manager. Let's rephrase that, by inner workings we don't mean coding talk, but talk about the progress and challenges in getting the coding done. This is where disconnected silos within a release project result in a reactive approach in finding out about coding issues, delays, re-works to the requirements, spec changes, etc The release manager not being in the loop increases their anxiety and results in chasing progress in meetings and emails.

Let's stop a minute and think about all the roles and silos the release manager is coordinating with during a release. And with that comes a lot of conversations and documentation that lives all over the place and is hard to find and thread together to make sense of. And then times this by four, given they are organising multiple releases in parallel. Ever tried to cook a meal when ingredients are in the wrong section in the pantry, some are missing, some are empty, some you ate yesterday...oops. Now imagine cooking multiple meals at the same time.

Let's just say organisation is key to a smooth-running kitchen and getting warm meals on tables. The last thing a chef wants to say is, 'I'm sorry sir, but that is no longer on the menu today.'

Preparation

The release manager's challenge is to oversee the development, testing, deployment, and support of software releases into operation and establish effective use of the service in order to deliver value to the customer.

But the way they operated as a team was a roadblock to potentially more effective deliveries. They had pain points in document disorganisation, frustration in scattered conversations and struggling to be aware of progress across the various roles involved in a release.

Their work is heavy on dependencies. A lack of awareness and misalignments caused pressure on team members and blew out delivery dates which ultimately had consequences for project delivery teams who are interfacing with customers awaiting a release. So, what did they want?

A central place for visibility of work, new behaviours for source of truth conversations and document versions, and trackable ways for progress. This not only streamlined the release management process and eased frustration - but enabled a potential to mitigate emerging issues, troubleshoot them with speed, and deliver on time.

The more visibility to observe the here and now, the more intel they had in delivering quality releases on time.

Guarantee - this meal will not cause the following side effects!

- We are struggling to agree on the specs on time as per the Release Calendar key dates. This is resulting in consumed effort for analysis instead of starting the release activities like writing technical design documents or doing coding

- During coding either the specs are changing by the clients or even from the development team because issues are detected where most of the times should have been caught during analysis. This is resulting in effort overruns or in rework
- We agree on a delivery date – then communications in email about change of date – but we don't have an official place to reflect the change of date, so some of us are not aligned
- We have a challenge in tracking how an item is progressing in our release management process. This results in wasted time chasing status on an item, searching my email inbox on what was agreed three months ago, or asking someone and waiting for answer… it's so frustrating
- I cannot be sure that what I'm holding in my hands is the latest integration specifications document – I find it difficult knowing the location of these documents and rely on specific people to retrieve them for me
- Each team member has a different understanding of what is the agreed scope and plan (depending on the meeting he/she participates). Now, imagine someone new joining mid-release, they would have no history or idea of what's been going on, there's no official place for our operations.

Ingredients

- Multiple Teams in Microsoft Teams
- Channels
- Tabs
- Files
- Planner
- OneNote

Method

There are four releases each year. A Team will be created to coordinate each release. Due to the work being coordinated across multiple releases a year in parallel – it's important each release has its own Team to avoid confusion. The Team template is as follow:

Eg. 2021R1 – Release Management

- Release Scope
- Technical Design
- QA Prep
- Coding
- Stability
- QA Execution
- Performance Testing
- General Availability
- Reporting (private)

Channels match the work priorities in getting a release into production – they represent official stages or components in the release management process. Some roles spend more time in one channel than another – but key here is that all channels are visible to all members. A coder or developer will not be too involved in the release scope channel, but just the same they have visibility into the workings in this channel. They can interact in this channel just the same. Here we are connecting or bridging the silos to make a more cohesive release management project. Given full visibility, we can reduce incidences of miscommunication, shifting problems from one area to the next, clashes, etc. And of course, the head chef, the release manager in our case, leverages this new visibility more than anyone in this Team.

Patterns
Across all these channels we identified three patterns of interaction in this Team – Inform & Proceed, Plan & Discuss, and Progress & Troubleshoot.

Simply put, this is what the members are spending their time doing in this Team.

The release manager will inform when each requirement is signed off, hence others can proceed to create their tasks. They will inform when all the requirements are signed off – this milestone is followed by informing the technical design can proceed, and again informing when it has been signed off. You can imagine all the other milestones of coding start/completed, available for deployment, stability start/completed, quality assurance signed off, and the announcement of general availability.

All members are aligned with official communications and dates, etc, no more miscommunications, hunting for information in your inbox – instead go to the source of truth and be informed in a flash.

If you were new to this Team or starting your role halfway through a release, you could self-serve the history of all the milestones and when they exactly happened.

Every announcement of a stage in the release is followed by a pattern of *plan & discuss*. Once the requirements, technical design, testing, etc are signed off – a whole lots of discussions start in planning the tasks, effort required and the resource allocation. These discussions (conversations, meetings) are now in the channels, and less of a black box. This visibility enables anyone, importantly the release manager to self-serve progress, rather than chasing people down. There's more confidence in the progress of things, more time in our day as information is easy to find, less emails and meetings overwhelming everyone as we can self-serve rather than chase, less re-works as we do things right the first time as we have visibility across silos, and of course a more proactive approach to see potential clashes and delays.

Throughout most stages of a release what follows all this planning and discussing is the pattern of *progress & troubleshoot*. Here we see the same benefits due to heightened visibility and the connecting of silos within a release. Coding delays and issues don't make the release manager's desk at a late hour, the release manager is observing work in progress and has more potential to see these things coming. And less of it is coming due to a more cohesive approach to teamwork. And it's not just being more in the know of the coding progress, but also the testing process and into production which is guaranteed to involve war room troubleshooting to nail every bug and last-minute issue.

Secret Sauce – @mention is a key feature for this team

Given planning and coordinating releases involves many roles – its essential members are notified about key messages for alignment.

But it's also essential that a member's activity feed doesn't get too overwhelmed with notifications from the interactions of one stage of a release that they may not be that involved in.

In addition to 'Member' and 'Team' mentions, we recommended 'Tag' mentions for specific scenarios to reduce the noise that comes with using @Team which notifies all Team members.

This is especially useful for stability conversations between devs and testers that can involve a myriad of conversations. Tag mentions enables members to not hesitate in their conversations and give them confidence they were not disrupting others.

Check for seasoning

So, let's take a look at what conversations this Team is cooking up

Release Manager – "Here is the Change Request form with the changes from yesterday's meeting"
- Reply by Quality Assurance – "Please open up a product backlog item for this"
- Reply by Release Officer – "The item has now been created for tasks and estimations"
- Conversations about tasks and estimations can continue with all roles in the loop and stored in the one place. Knowing this information as it happens enables the Release Manager to more effectively understand how the effort and allocation of pending work will affect milestones and scheduling

Product Developer – "What's the progress of the API on this item"

- Reply by Developer – "it will be one week late is that ok"
- Release Manager now privy to these conversations has intel to see how this may affect release outcomes and chime in if required. Prior to having this visibility, the Release Manager may find out things too late.

Acceptance testing – "Item 156 statistics error - customer told me that...."

- Followed by 50 replies of problem solving
- All Team members including the release manager can see the progress and solution estimations of current issues and bugs without having to chase for this information as they did in the past

Many of these examples would have previously been an email between a couple of people, but now it's visible to all in the Team. Not only from a conversation history point of view to look back at the past to see the conversations behind decisions, but also to have one source of truth conversation in the here and now to prevent duplication, miscommunication, unseen dependencies, delays.

So, how's your meal?

To deliver meals on time to customers requires a well-oiled coordination approach across the different roles in the kitchen. In our case "I'll know this is successful when we have a leaner effort rate by doing the same with less, improving quality by reducing the number of defects, and hitting milestones on schedule and time." In practice this is translates to:

- Reducing occurrences of revisiting effort estimations after already starting the technical design
- Reducing occurrences of revisiting technical design after already starting the coding process
- Reducing the time, it takes to retrieve the latest conversation about our effort estimations or about testing our code stability
- Having confidence that I'm looking at the latest version of a customer analysis file – and with the confidence that I'm not missing any stray conversations.

For a team with a high-level of interdependencies this new and improved approach indeed feels as satisfying as eating 'soft serve' – I told you I'd come back to this!

A LEADERSHIP HUB TO MANAGE CLINICS ACROSS A REGION

As a regional manager accountable for the operations of multiple medical clinics, it can be a daunting role simply managing and keeping track of all the communications and information exchanged with clinic staff. These conversations happen across multiple spinning plates in the regional manager's kitchen. Some of the dishes served on these plates are about engagement, profitability, safety, productivity, patient experiences, customer growth and loyalty, etc. And as much as a regional manager is doing all the right things and covering all the bases required to run a successful region (or kitchens), it's another thing dealing with the communication overwhelm in keeping up with the ins and outs of what's in motion without a few plates breaking. And I know what you are thinking – Greek restaurants break a lot of plates. Yes, but they do this intentionally as part of their entertainment. The difference here is that a regional manager is not intentionally breaking plates. It is not really a show they'd like to put on. Let's think of it with this visual.

If a plate is spinning fast enough – it has stability. And if this spin slows too much, we have instability. And let's say for our context that – low visibility of the work going on in your region leads to instability.

If this were an applied maths class, we would say – the rate of spin of a plate is proportional to the visibility of the plate.

So, if a regional manager (or head chef) has low visibility to self-serve progress of a piece of work (i.e. a particular plate), then this low visibility of work as it unfolds becomes drag on that spin.

In our case, it was being faced with low situational awareness of what's happening today and this week across all the clinics under their leadership. They simply didn't have a good enough view of the weekly progress of middle management. Their method of keeping the spin rate going was to send emails and make phone calls to know what's going on or call a meeting when the spin became a sure wobble.

Our aim was to set-up this head chef and their team with the behaviours and technologies to make the "wobbles" a thing of the past, and to reduce their overhead of wasted time and reputational risk in sweeping shards of broken plates from the kitchen floor.

Preparation

One of differentiators of a humming kitchen comes from the top-down house rules. The kitchens that operate well, operate as a team. And this starts from the huddle in the kitchen where the head-chef outlines the processes and behaviours for a fluid operation. Now I'm thinking this is where we can stop the metaphor as I'm not sure of many head-chefs (sorry if I'm wrong) that allow for user-input into how they work as a team. But yes, we believe there also needs to be a bottom-up inclusive approach where members of the team can express their experiences and needs so all is catered for a well-oiled machine.

Our current head-chef (regional manager) had not yet taken the time as a group to decide on their teamwork processes, protocols, and behaviours. So, people resorted to what they know – send emails and have lots of meetings. And we know this is not elegant enough of a design to align with the practice of effective 'group work'.

An unconsidered approach to group work for this team resulted in being too re-active in chasing status and putting out fires, not enough thought about who needs to be involved and who it's going to impact, no source of truth and its consequences when going off out-dated documentation and conversations, and slow decision-making due to the time it takes to canvas past and present interactions.

But this was to change as the regional manager gathered all their people to co-design a way forward. Re-examining their teamwork processes and tools would be the first step to sustain a good spin rate on all their spinning plates.

Their goal was to improve the frequency and visibility of communication with their direct reports:

- To be more aware of progress between meetings – by having one place for leadership/management to communicate, align, and share progress.

- For their work to be organised by topic so they can find something quickly.

A visible place that gives confidence no-one is missing out and reduces the need of repeating the same information.

Guarantee - this meal will not cause the following side effects!

- I get 100+ emails a day. I'm drowning in email. I have no idea that the 56th email in my inbox is the one I should have read first. And I spend too much time and frustration looking through past emails to weave a picture together

- I'm always repeating the same information and conversations. Either a person can't find what I said in the mess of their inbox, or they heard something based on a conversation I had with another manager. We need to make these conversations more visible so others can come across them in their own time or be brought into the conversation

- We are simply not aligned on discussions – for example some clinics are doing things different ways with current billing practices. Sometimes this is bad, sometimes it's good in that other clinics could benefit from doing the same

- As for our projects and initiatives – when I send an important email, I'm not confident it has been read, I don't know if it has been actioned or the latest progress. I must search for an answer, elicit a response, ask around for an update – it's all very time consuming. Within a minute I want to be able to know exactly where I am on a project and what's outstanding. I spend so much time doing this to prepare for national meetings with my peers

- When I finally locate one of our procedures, I have very low confidence if it's the latest or official one. And it's not just procedures, it's also our daily documentation. Going by the wrong version can cause operational issues. We've had occurrences where going off an old version of a staffing roster has negatively impacted the call centres when booking patients *'Oh, sorry we thought the doctor who can do dopplers was in today, but it turns out they are not rostered today.'* This doesn't go well with patients going through a hard time in their life.

Ingredients

- Microsoft Teams
- Channels
- Tabs
- Files
- Planner
- OneNote

Method

It is hard to manage when you can't see what's going on. Visibility is king. And the biggest culprit of making work invisible is email – which caused plates to wobble for this team.

Email is private or exclusive by default. Unless you are in the email you are not in the club of knowing what's going on. Shifting to a more public and inclusive space for conversations and content allowed this teams work to be visible and observed. And what this means for both members and the regional manager is that information doesn't need to be repeated, you don't need to be clairvoyant of who needs to know something as they can have access and read up for themselves, you see things coming and take pro-active measures, and you are more aligned on what's going on.

The solution was to have one place/one conversation for leadership and middle management to communicate, align, and share progress.

The outcome would improve their currency and situational awareness to ensure there is more member cohesiveness and interactions around their end goals and team activities

This was a shift to a self-serve model. Work is visible online, and you visit to inform yourself – reducing the 'chasing for progress' syndrome.

Microsoft Teams and associated apps were the technology to make this happen

Let's get into the details of how to cook this recipe. The key activities covered in this Team:

- Documentation was to inform members correctly

- The regional manager would post updates about how clinics were going and productivity, and asking questions about improving performance

- Project work would be done in other Teams. This Team would be used to update the regional manager of the latest on projects (Note: that the regional manager has access to various project Teams and can observe for himself if need be)

  - Cross-functional in the loop messaging about auditing, compliance, testing, servicing, down times.

Without further ado, the Team:

Region 4 Leadership Hub
- Staffing and rostering
- Equipment
- Clinic performance
- Marketing
- Workplace H&S

- Projects
- Billing

Let's look at a few of these priorities (i.e. Channels)

Staffing and rostering

There's now confidence in accessing the latest version of a roster – and quickly via the tab. It is not in an email attachment, it's not in a shared drive, it's not in someone's OneDrive. Instead, it's in an agreed communal space. They are all operating from the same book.

A post is made with the dates a doctor/nurse is available and in the thread there's a discussion and approval of those dates that gives the go-ahead to update the roster. Patients can be booked on the right days according to the type of medical professional required. This type of thing happens daily/weekly.

If someone is wondering about a specific entry on the roster, they can look to the past conversations to see why that decision was made.

But it's not just about accessing the roster or getting approval to ink people into the roster. It is also about the frequent changes that happen. Doctors/Nurses call in sick or they are re-assigned to other priorities. Now conversations about these movements happen in real-time and patients can either be re-booked as soon as possible, or if there's capacity staff can switch between clinics to fill the gaps. No-one is ever left in the dark, the conversation thread grows as movement happens.

And of course, it's not just about scheduling, but also recruitment and forecasting of staff requirements ahead – whether it's staff on leave, an attrition of professionals with a particular skill, an introduction to new staff and their skillsets, etc

Clinic Performance / Equipment
These channels are used to inform members of dates when performance and compliance testing will be done. Often conversations about test date changes occur so rostering and patient bookings can align.

Results of tests are shared in the replies to inform members of whether this impacts present and future bookings.

The above is the same with equipment that goes down. Updates are shared about fix times and when things will resume.

Let's recall that before working a new way with Teams – a member may not be privy to equipment notices. Or they weren't updated at the micro level as they are now. If one member needed to chase something they would call or email. And the problem lies that the other members who also may have the same question were not part of this conversation. And of course, the scenario where individuals email the same question.

Circling back on house rules

Throwing new technology to old processes isn't going to necessarily make things more visible overnight. What's important is to nurture behaviours for the team to work more observably – otherwise there's nothing to witness.

Here are some of the principles of the kitchen to get hot meals to customers every time

- Expectation to check-in at the beginning and throughout the day

- If a status changes on an equipment update leave a reply and re-edit the subject heading

- Emails will be replied to in Teams (unless not relevant to the wider group)

- Do not email before, during, after meeting, as we will use the meeting post for conversations and OneNote for meeting notes

- Only @mention the regional manager if the post requires their attention or action

- Important messages require a 'like', so leadership understands it has been read (and they require a reply if been asked)

- Recording and shared minutes for those that often can't make a meeting

Secret Sauce – Cross-functional awareness

The real game changer was the cross-functional messaging. By that we mean people from different roles participating in the same space. Knowing what's happening in one function of the business, enabled another function to plan better or make more informed decisions. Previously it was a black box to staff about what happened in the last hour with the equipment's team. Now Marketing can understand why a clinic is quiet so they can book correctly. If a piece of medical equipment is down, then bookings would alert others and divert them to another clinic. Now all are in the know of follow-up actions – they know the equipment is down, but they also know that an engineer has been contacted, and soon they'll know that the engineer is in the building, etc

Check for seasoning

Every team is different. In professional services often it's asking a question or advice – has anyone worked with this customer before, does anyone have experience with this, etc.

The key pattern in this Team is posting 'updates.' The 'here and now' and speed to get things back on track is important to this team. If they are not good at keeping each other informed and in the loop, it's the patient that gets the short straw. Some examples of typical updates:

- We need to confirm a registered nurse today, otherwise we need to cancel present appointments. I've talked to Joe, so we know what's ok to do without a nurse
- Compliance testing will take place on the CT equipment in the city clinic this Wednesday
- The radiographer is sick today in the city clinic – I have Thomas from the west city clinic to cover
- Our 6-monthly WHS audit is now complete for the city clinic
- A scheduled test was performed on the MRI in the city clinic yesterday – no impact on patient workflow. Service report available here
- We have a nursing shortage – I've escalated this to recruitment who are expanding the search to locum agencies, hospitals, etc We are currently waiting for a call back from two people. I will let everyone know as soon as possible if this changes and, in the meantime, we will need to make the necessary adjustment to next week's schedules
- We have an experienced nurse coming from the city – she has oncology, radiotherapy and acute care experience. She will start on Wednesday which

gives us time to walk her through our procedures and environment.

Yep, it seems the taste testing is over. This meal is ready to serve to all members.

So, how's your meal?

For the recipe to taste right we had to hit this goal: "I'll know this is successful when we can make speedier decisions as it will be more visible to find information that has already been discussed about a topic, and progress."

We'll improve our currency and situational awareness to ensure there is more member cohesiveness and interactions around our end goals and team activities. We now have:

- One source of truth information for operational activities (no more confusion/uncertainty) e.g., staffing and bookings

- Proactive updating by members so we are more cohesive with each other's actions

- More visibility in current conversations and content to make quicker and informed decisions

- To easily know the progress/resolved actions or completed protocols

- To get our time back (less making sense of situations, less email to go through)

This meal indeed tastes like it sounded on the menu. Now, what's for dessert?

Kitchen Talk

For those uninitiated in online work group spaces, it may seem quite bewildering that access to more information would not just compound the existing problem of communication overwhelm. It does seem quite magical for this team:

- They are more informed of what's going on without the expense of being constantly pinged

- The past is kindly woven into threads within topic areas for super quick retrieval

- They gain some time back in their day and yet have even more situational awareness

- And this is the same experience for everyone, not just the regional manager.

But how is this kitchen wizardry so?!

It is all in the design – using the channels functionality in Teams. This team has seven shared inboxes i.e. channels (one for each priority area of work)

When a new message comes in, it's posted into one of the seven inboxes (i.e. Channels)

When the regional manager has their second sip of coffee in the morning they may see – three new items in the Marketing channel, two in the Equipment channel, one in the Projects channel, etc. In this way they can choose where they want to put their focus. Whereas in email they may have to go through many emails before getting to those marketing emails they were looking to focus on.

Now I know what you are saying – what if there's an urgent matter in a channel they are not focusing in?

So, let's backtrack – we talked about their second sip of coffee, but what are they doing on their first sip of coffee?

As they get their first hit of coffee, they are looking in their Teams activity feed. This is the priority inbox of them all. This is the nirvana inbox. The activity feed has notifications to all the conversations the regional manager is in across all the Teams they are joined to. This is where they are notified of new replies to their posts, replies to other people's posts they have replied in, and posts where their name has been mentioned. Imagine every email in your inbox was only about stuff you need to pay attention to and action, and all the rest of the emails lived outside of your main inbox. This is the activity feed!

Now there's no more new items in the Equipment channel. Why? The regional manager's name was mentioned in those two items, so they read them in their activity feed and dealt with them.

But there's still one new item in the Project channel and three new items in the Marketing channel, given these items were not replies to their posts or did not mention their name – which means it's good to know information and they will get to it when they can. On this occasion the regional manager spent the next while looking at those new items in the Marketing channel.

Hopefully, it's become apparent that the regional manager is in charge of their information processing and not the other way around. We can see this is not magic, but good design.

- They are more informed of what's going on without the expense of being constantly pinged

  - Eg. Those three posts in the Marketing channels did not ping their Activity feed, but yet they are visible and accessible to look at when the time is right for them. This can be the difference between chasing someone for progress tomorrow by sending yet another email, or reading about that progress made the day before in a post

- The past is kindly woven into threads within topic areas for super quick retrieval

    o Eg. At any time, they can go to the Billings channel to look at the history of conversations. Usually, most team members would create their own email folders to file their conversations by topic – whereas now those conversations are born in those topic areas

- They gain some time back in their day and yet have even more situational awareness

    o Eg. When you can get to what matters quicker, find content in a flash, and self-serve awareness – there's more time to get stuff done.

Too much salt!

We are not going to withhold this important fact – and it comes down to the house rules and behaviours set in each Team. The nirvana inbox i.e. the activity feed has the potential to become polluted. This can happen when the regional manager's name is mentioned in posts that don't really require their action. That is why this regional manager set the rule to please only mention their name in a post if it requires their attention or action. If their name is not mentioned, they will still get round to reading those messages, but just not as a priority.

Hence, why we discussed earlier in this piece – throwing new technology alone at a team will not necessarily improve all your teamwork woes. It is taking the opportunity to re-examine the processes and behaviours that are to wrap around that technology that is going to make the 100% difference.

YOUR NEXT STEPS

The purpose of this book wasn't to give you the definitive procedural steps to get the most out of Office 365. On the contrary, our goal was to equip you with understanding, awareness, and inspiration that will enable you and your team to do amazing things, empowered by the technology at your fingertips.

We know from our work with executives, managers, team leaders, and those on the front line, it takes more than reading a book, watching a video, or attending a workshop to build your proficiency and confidence in this area. It takes time. It takes practice. It takes commitment.

Just like an apprentice chef embarking on their career, it takes commitment to building your knowledge, to exploring new ingredients, to experiencing new flavours. It also takes the experience of someone who has mastered some of those ingredients, skills, and recipes to guide you in the right direction.

By reading this book, you have insight to some of the experiences that we, the co-authors of this book bring to the table. We are not the only people you should look to though.

Be an apprentice

Within almost every organisation we work with, there are a handful of people who impress us so much. They have two attributes that we admire. First, they have mastery of many of the topics we introduced you to in this book. They are digitally fluent, and confident in the application of their skills across Office 365. Second, they have mastery of their role, their process, or their industry. A beautiful mix of digital capability, and business know how that makes an individual almost unstoppable.

Our ask of you is simple. Seek out these individuals in your organisation. Get to know them. Look to see if there are opportunities for you to work with them or be mentored by them. Their guidance will take you from good... to great.

... or take one under your wing

If on the off chance you are that individual, we ask that you lead this conversation within your organisation – a focus on building the confidence of your workforce when it comes to using digital tools. This doesn't mean running a large-scale training program... it means guiding people through solving real business problems or improving work practices. Actionable advice. Generous guidance. Reducing the overwhelm that technology and 'hybrid work' places on us all. In the spirit of 'paying it forward'.

Gourmet Teamwork is not all that meaningful if you are the only member of the team. The future of work is a team sport... but your playing field is across your city, across your country, or across the globe. It is within your team, across teams, or across organisations.

Reading this book is the first step. Continue to get to know your ingredients, continue to develop those skills, and continue to explore new recipes with your peers. Together, you are on your way to reimagining work in a way that helps you achieve your professional, and personal goals. Congratulations on making the next step in your (Office 365 inspired) 'culinary journey'.

ABOUT THE AUTHORS

Paul Woods

 Paul Woods is the General Manager of the Adopt & Embrace team at Rapid Circle. The Adopt & Embrace team focuses on helping people get their day back through sustainable, relevant, and focused adoption of Microsoft 365 that results in real business outcomes.

Prior to their acquisition by Rapid Circle in July 2021, Adopt & Embrace was announced as a finalist the Employee Experience category of the 2021 Microsoft Global Partner of the Year awards. In 2018, Adopt & Embrace was recognised as a Microsoft Global Partner of the year after just two years and nine months of operation.

Before staring Adopt & Embrace in 2015, Paul held various marketing and management roles at a major

Australian Microsoft Partner and was a Technology Specialist at Microsoft Australia. He recently completed research as part of the Work/Industry Futures Research Program at the Queensland University of Technology, focusing on technology-enabled mobile work and the porosity of work/life borders. He has also been a member of the teaching team at the QUT Business School for Strategic Management and Negotiation Across Borders.

Awarded Microsoft's Most Valuable Professional (MVP) award ten times, Paul is a regular speaker at community-based events as well as at regional and global Microsoft Conferences like Microsoft TechEd, Microsoft Ignite: The Tour, and Microsoft Inspire.

Find him on Twitter as @paulwoods or on LinkedIn at https://www.linkedin.com/in/paulwoods.

Helen Blunden

 Helen Blunden is the Community Manager for Rapid Circle and has many years' experience of learning and development across private, public and not-for-profit organisations. With a specialty in

performance consulting and informal learning, she believes that organisations need to help their employees build new skills to navigate through a complex world of change.

Helen has a passion for enabling people to learn beyond traditional tools. She believes in the power of networks and communities that are supported by social tools that drive collaboration, meaning, and engagement in work.

Helen believes that "learning is the work, and the work is the learning," meaning that the tools are the instruments that enable us to connect with peers who can inspire us with fresh new ideas, allowing us to apply them in our own unique ways either for personal or professional contexts. She has a passion for showing people ways to inspire learning experiences in everything they do. At a practical level, she has experience with all forms of facilitator-led instruction, online, blended, social and virtual, and she practices what she preaches. She is an active user of a variety of tools and emerging technologies that she uses regularly for her own personal learning journeys as well as assist with her clients and communities. Find her on Twitter as @activatelearn on or LinkedIn where she regularly shares her thinking and resources.

Aditi Gupta

 Aditi is an Adoption Consultant with Rapid Circle. She has over 12 years of systems strategy and adoption experience in roles across ICT, Telco, Finance, and Health, with particular focus on driving strategic system enhancements and capabilities, playing various customer facing roles globally.

Prior to that, Aditi was a successful entrepreneur having owned and managed a small Brisbane-based health business, where she combined her love for mindset coaching, a passion she pursues in her free time to help people become their best self-fulfilled version, along with training and nutrition. She strongly believes in harnessing the power of their own minds to help people achieve long lasting results. Self-acceptance informs her coaching style as she sees herself as a continual work in progress, but with compassion.

John Tropea

John is an Adoption Consultant at Rapid Circle. He has spent the last 4 years working on projects with a diverse set of clients in Mining, Health, Education, and Retail. The projects have ranged from organisational wide programs to impact engagement and culture, to working with departments and small groups  to improve teamwork behaviours and processes. The approach is high on stakeholder engagement to make change and new ways of working meaningful and practical, and then coaching to onboard new behaviours and habits.

Earlier endeavours have been in the similar user experience spaces, as a Communities of Practice Manager, Document Management Specialist and Corporate Librarian. You may still find John wearing a cardigan today brewing pour-over coffee whilst listening to his favourite ambient music cassette.

Jeff Bell

Jeff is a Senior Adoption Consultant at Rapid Circle. Having over 25 years in the ICT industry Jeff has a raft of experience in dealing with change and supporting staff. Experiences range from being on a Help Desk to managing and delivering project deliverables to supporting the project and affected by staff via training and development and change management practices. Jeff's focus is always ensuring staff benefit from using the underpinning technology that's aligned to their processes. Whether this is getting their lunch break back, exceeding their teams KPIs or working towards delivering the organisations targets.

Jenni McNamara

Jenni is a Senior Adoption Consultant with Rapid Circle. With over 30 years' experience as a corporate Coach, Facilitator and Technology Trainer.

Jenni is passionate about enhancing collaboration, communication and coordination across organisations through effective implementation and adoption strategies using Microsoft 365 technologies, across diverse corporate industries like Legal, Finance and Mining.

Jenni as has always been focused on helping others to find ways to work smarter not harder. She is people focused with a track record for implementing and improving processes and procedures.

Her firsthand experience using the office suite to deliver high quality outcomes built a reputation as a go to person for productivity and efficiency techniques.

Find her on LinkedIn where she regularly shares her tips and tricks.